Value Investing

"All intelligent investing is values investing acquiring more that you are paying for. You must value the business in order to value the stock."

-- *Charlie* Munger

Vivek Choudhary

To My Hero Warren Buffett, Benjamin Graham, David Dodd, Charles Munger, J. K. Rowling, Bruce Greenwald, Tano Santos & To You.

PREFACE

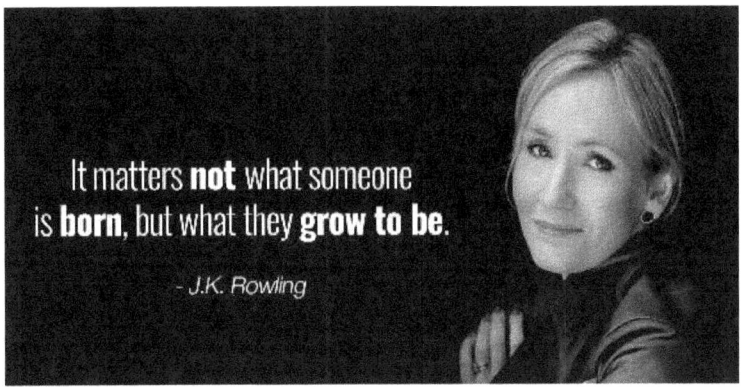

To be a value investor it requires lots of Patience and Humility, this book is what I believe in and using the valuation process is the heart of value investing, I am quite lucky to come across, to learn value investing and now I practice it, I strict to the principal of the value investing framework, "All I want to know is where I'm going to die, so I'll never go there." Charlie Munger. A good value investor read a lot because one should be updated about the market as well as about the company where they are investing in, I love to read, reading is one of the best things I do, and reading helps me to be updated in my field. I think all of the value investors read a lot, in value investing knowledge plays a critical role in your investment to be successful.

I am practicing value investing and buying securities from the last two decades and when I come across value investing through reading about Warren Buffett.

I think value investing is a secret to find good company and to systematic analysis with all the information and value the company, I can say above all the investing book you have read so far, this book will create enormous wealth for you once you start using the process of value investing, I have to use the real-world case study of Apple, the stock I bought at $ 170 in 2018 and the price move to $332 in 2019, with 95.29% growth in a year, don't think it is strange when you will become value investor, it will be possible for you too, all you need a right valuation, right risk management tool and strict discipline, your attitude towards your goal is determine by yourself as said by great writer all time J.K. Rowling "it matters not what someone is born, but what they grow to be ".I wish all of you reading this book will fulfil your purpose and increase your net worth, I don't have doubts about it, Applying value investing people have become wealthy like warren Buffett and lots other in different parts of the world , when I buy the stock using the value investing framework, I am rest assured about my return and investment, there is no doubts that I will not make money, as said by Warren Buffett

"I always knew I was going to be rich. I don't think I ever doubted it for a minute"

Always look for a good company which has a barrier to entry and economic moats, in this book you will learn about Assets Value (AV), Earning Power Value (EPV) and Franchise Value (FV) and then you will learn how to do strategic analysis of a company and at last about the risk management tool, most important, try not to lose your money, you have to preserve your capital. I try to write the book in a very plain and simple way so that you can easily understand and use it for your capital appreciation, all the best for your future endeavour.

Introduction

Value investing is a process , the process that combine two ingredients to be successful , a good understanding economic of the business operation , the company and their study and a discipline valuation approach , this two things have to integrated , in this book you will learn how to do this integration successfully , first we understand assets value then we move to earning power value , then we ask yourself does this company enjoy barriers to entry or not ?once we get the answer then we go to the next step to analyse the franchise value of the company , if the answer is no then we stop going forward , organising the information in a structural way ,there are still lots of information need to be collect , but we are interested in one thing , do we want to buy this company or not ?do we want to be a shareholders or ? that the kind of approach we value investor look for in buying any company ,deep understanding of the company operating and performance , that too company should be within our circle of competence , once you will have deep understanding of the company , the you will check the margin of the safety , whether we have sufficient margin of safety or not and the long horizon outlook and use key risk analysis tool to understand your capital profit or not , do the earning is sustainable and will always support barrier to entry , to be a successful value investor three things to be integrated , a good understanding of company , the valuation approach and risk management tools can lead you to be creating enormous wealth in investing world , now welcome to the world of value investing , let start the journey .....

About the Author

Vivek Choudhary is a Value Investor & Entrepreneur who has over 20 years of experience in investment and entrepreneurship. Involve in diversify business Commodities, Manufacturing, Hotel & Automobiles.

He earned MBA in finance & Marketing at IIPM, MDP in Strategic Market Planning at IIM, Equity Research Analyst at BSE Institute, Value Investing at Stanford University Continue studies, and Entrepreneurship

Essential & Leading with Finance at HBX Harvard Business School & Value Investing at Columbia Business School, Business Lesson Cohort at Harvard Business School Online.

He is passionate about Value Investing and invests globally. His hobby is reading. He reads everyday, value investing books and finance books.

He admires his Hero Mr. Warren Buffett Chief Executive Officer of Berkshire Hathaway – He follows his footprint of Value Investing. For him reading and studying are like compounding, it will help him in achieving his passion.

He wrote the book

- **Value Investing & Behavioral Finance**

- **Wealth Creation & Financial Statement Analysis "Dream to be Wealthy"**

- **Value Investing - Legendary Graham & Dodd Valuation**

- **Value Investing CHECKLIST**

CONTENTS

Preface   III

Introduction   VI

Value Investing History   1

1. Ben Graham   2
2. David Dodd   14
3. Bruce Greenwald   19
4. Warren Buffett   21
5. Charles Munger   29
   - Causes of Human Misjudgement   36

Introduction to Value Investing   49

6. Value Investing   50
   - Three Principal of Value Investing   56
   - Reason to be a Value investor   65
   - How to be a Good Value investor   67
   - What Requires to a Good Value Investor   68
   - Be successful Value investor   70

CONTENTS

- **7.** Process of value Investing — 72
  - Search Good Stock — 73
    - Institutional Bias — 76
    - Individual Bias — 76
- **8.** Valuation — 80
  - Drawback of Relative valuation — 81
  - Drawback of Discounted cash Flow — 82
  - Three Element to value a business — 90
    - Asset Value (AV)
    - Earnings Power Value (EPV)
    - Franchise Value (FV)
- **9.** Barriers to Entry — 98
  - Compare Assets Value with Earning Power Value.
- **10.** The Framework of Value Investing — 106
- **11.** Valuation of Apple Inc — 124
  - Assets Value — 127
  - Earning Power Value — 138
- **12.** EV/EBITDA vs. EV/GP — 165
- **13.** Franchise Value — 172
  - Barrier to entry
    - Supply Based
    - Demand Based
  - Not a Barrier to entry

CONTENTS

14. Competitive Advantage	183
15. Three Step Strategic Analyses	188
o The Firm	191
o The Industry	204
o Value Chain	225
16. Debts & Cash	229
17. Risk Management	231
o Stock	233
o Portfolio	243
o Macroeconomics	247
18. Important note for Value Investor	252

Value Investing History

"Read 500 pages...every day. That's how knowledge works. It builds up, like compound interest. All of you can do it, but I guarantee not many of you will do it."

-Warren Buffett

1
Ben Graham

Benjamin Graham

Graham reading an edition of *Moody's Manual*, 1955

Born	Benjamin Grossbaum May 9, 1894 London, England, UK
Died	September 21, 1976 (aged 82) Aix-en-Provence, France
Nationality	American
Institution	Columbia University University of California, Los Angeles
Alma mater	Columbia University
Contributions	*Security Analysis* (1934) *The Intelligent Investor* (1949) Benjamin Graham formula

The "father of value investing"

Benjamin Graham (May 9, 1894 – September 21, 1976) was a British-born American investor, economist, and professor. He is widely known as the "father of value investing", and wrote two of the founding texts in neoclassical investing: Security Analysis (1934) with David Dodd, and The Intelligent Investor (1949). His investment philosophy stressed investor psychology, minimal debt, buy-and-hold investing, and fundamental analysis, concentrated diversification, buying within the margin of safety, activist investing, and contrarian mindsets.

After graduating from Columbia University at age 20, he started his career on Wall Street, eventually founding the Graham-Newman Partnership. After employing his former student Warren Buffett, he took up teaching positions at his alma mater, and later at UCLA Anderson School of Management at the University of California, Los Angeles.

His work in managerial economics and investing has led to a modern wave of value investing within mutual funds, hedge funds, diversified holding companies, and other investment vehicles. Throughout his career, Graham had many notable disciples who went on to receive substantial success in the world of investment, including Irving Kahn and Buffett, the latter going on to describe him as the second most influential person in his life after his own father; both would name a child after Graham, another one of Graham's famous students was Sir John Templeton.

An early copy of Graham's Intelligent Investor

His first book, Security Analysis with David Dodd, was published in 1934, In Security Analysis; he proposed a clear definition of investment that was distinguished from what he deemed speculation. It read, *An investment operation is one which, upon thorough analysis, promises safety of principal and an adequate return. Operations not meeting these requirements are speculative."*

Warren Buffett describes The Intelligent Investor (1949) as *"the best book about investing ever written."* Graham exhorted the stock market participant to first draw a fundamental distinction between investment and speculation.

Graham wrote that the owner of equity stocks should regard them first and foremost as conferring part ownership of a business. With that perspective in mind, the stock owner should not be too concerned with erratic fluctuations in stock prices, since in the short term the stock market behaves like a voting machine, but in the long term it acts like a weighing machine (i.e. its true value will be reflected in its stock price in the long run). Graham distinguished between the passive and the active investor. The passive investor, often referred to as a defensive investor, invests cautiously, looks for value stocks, and buys for the long term. The active investor, on the other hand, is one who has more time, interest, and possibly more specialized knowledge to seek out exceptional buys in the market. Graham recommended that investors spend time and effort to analyze the financial state of companies. When a company is available on the market at a price which is at a discount to its intrinsic value, a "margin of safety" exists, which makes it suitable for investment.

Graham wrote that investment is most intelligent when it is most business like. By that he meant that the stock investor is neither right nor wrong because others agreed or disagreed with him; he is right because his facts and analysis are right. Graham's favourite allegory is that of Mr. Market, a fellow who turns up every day at the stock holder's door offering to buy or sell his shares at a different price. Usually, the price quoted by Mr. Market seems plausible, but occasionally it is ridiculous. The investor is free to either agree with his quoted price and trade with him, or to ignore him completely. Mr. Market doesn't mind this, and will be back the following day to quote another price. The point is that the investor should not regard the whims of Mr. Market as determining the value of the shares that the investor owns. He should profit from market folly rather than participate in it. The investor is best off concentrating on the real life performance of his companies and receiving dividends, rather than being too concerned with Mr. Market's often irrational behaviour.

Graham was critical of the corporations of his day for obfuscated and irregular financial reporting that made it difficult for investors to discern the true state of the business's finances. He was an advocate of dividend payments to shareholders rather than businesses keeping all of their profits as retained earnings. He also criticized those who advised that some types of stocks were a good buy at any price, because of the prospect of sustained stock price growth, without a good analysis of the business's actual financial condition. These observations remain relevant today.

Graham's average investment performance was 20% annualized return over 1936 to 1956. The overall market performance for the same time period was 12.2% annually on average.

Graham's largest gain was from GEICO, which his Graham-Newman Partnership purchased 50% of in 1948 for $712,000. The position grew to $400 million by 1972, contributing more to the portfolio than all of Graham-Newman's other investments combined. GEICO was eventually acquired in whole by Berkshire Hathaway in 1996, having previously been saved by Buffett and John J. Byrne in 1976.

According to Graham and Dodd, value investing is deriving the intrinsic value of a common stock independent of its market price. By using a company's factors such as its assets, earnings, and dividend payouts, the intrinsic value of a stock can be found and compared to its market value. If the intrinsic value is more than the current price, the investor should buy and hold until a mean reversion occurs. A mean reversion is the theory that over time, the market price and intrinsic price will converge towards each other until the stock price reflects its true value. By buying an undervalued stock, the investor is, in effect, paying less for it and should sell when the price is trading at its intrinsic worth. This effect of price convergence is only bound to happen in an efficient market.

Graham was a strong proponent of efficient markets. If markets were not efficient, then the point of value investing will be pointless as the fundamental principle of value investments lies in the ability of the markets to eventually correct to their intrinsic values. Common stocks are not going to remain inflated or bottomed-out forever despite the irrationality of investors in the market.

Benjamin Graham noted that due to the irrationality of investors, including other factors such as the inability to predict the future and the fluctuations of the stock market, buying undervalued or out-of-favor stocks is sure to provide a margin of safety, i.e. room for human error, for the investor. Also, investors can achieve a margin of safety by purchasing stocks in companies with high dividend yields and low debt-to-equity ratios, and diversifying their portfolios. In the event that a company goes bankrupt, the margin of safety would mitigate the losses that the investor would have. Graham normally bought stocks trading at two-thirds their net-net value as his margin of safety cushion.

The original Benjamin Graham Formula for finding the intrinsic value of a stock was:

$$V = EPS \times (8.5 + 2g)$$

where:

V = intrinsic value

EPS = trailing 12-mth EPS of the company

8.5 = P/E ratio of a zero-growth stock

g = long-term growth rate of the company

In 1974, the formula was revised to include both a risk-free rate of 4.4% which was the average yield of high grade corporate bonds in 1962 and the current yield on AAA corporate bonds represented by the letter Y:

V=YEPS × (8.5 + 2g) × 4.4

Example Apple Inc

Earnings Per Share (EPS)	12.58 $
Projected Growth Rate (%)	5
Corporate Bond Yield (%)	2.53
Intrinsic Value of a Share	404.75 $

The Graham number is a figure that measures a stock's fundamental value by taking into account the company's earnings per share and book value per share. The Graham number is the upper bound of the price range that a defensive investor should pay for the stock. According to the theory, any stock price below the Graham number is considered undervalued and thus worth investing in. The formula is as follows:

$$\sqrt{22.5 \times (\text{earnings per share}) \times (\text{book value per share})}$$

Example Apple Inc

EPS = 12.58

BVPS= $20.60

The Intrinsic Value = $76

If the earning per share for a single share of company Apple Inc is $12.58, the book value per share is $20.6, the Graham number would be $76. (22.5*12.58*20.60)= $76, $76 is the maximum an investor should pay for a share of Apple Inc.

In Chapter 14 of "The Intelligent Investor Graham recommended requirements for the Defensive Investor, those criteria are as follows:

1. Adequate size of the enterprise
2. A sufficiently strong financial condition
3. Earnings stability
4. Dividend record
5. Earnings growth
6. Moderate price / Earnings ratio
7. Moderate ratio of price to assets

Value investing in Benjamin Graham and David Dodd's time emphasized four main ideas as follows: -

Intrinsic Value - any corporate security has an Intrinsic Value or in finance, intrinsic value or fundamental value is the "true, inherent, and essential value" of an asset independent of its market value, value which is justified by facts (assets, earnings, dividends and prospects).

Margin of Safety - Margin of safety is the difference between the intrinsic value of a stock and its market price. The lower the price of the security relative to its intrinsic value, the higher the Margin of Safety is.

Mr. Market - Mr. Market is an allegory created by investor Benjamin Graham to describe what he believed were the irrational or contradictory traits of the stock market and the risks of following groupthink, you should view market prices as if being in business with a manic-depressive partner. Repeatedly your partner offers to either sell or buy shares at prices strongly linked with his mental state at each time, ranging everywhere from highly pessimistic to wildly optimistic.

Diversification - Portfolio diversification is the risk management strategy of combining a variety of assets to reduce the overall risk of an investment portfolio, for risk management purposes you should carry at least 30 different stocks at each time.

2

David Dodd

David Dodd

David Dodd (ca. 1948), taken by Emanuel "Manny" Warman (1915–1983), Columbia University's official photographer for 37 years (courtesy of Columbia University Archives)

Born	August 23, 1895 Berkeley County, West Virginia, U.S.
Died	September 18, 1988 (aged 93) Portland, Maine, U.S.
Nationality	United States
Alma mater	University of Pennsylvania Columbia University
Known for	*Security Analysis*
Spouse(s)	Elsie Marguerite Firor
Scientific career	
Fields	Investment management, Economics
Institutions	Columbia Business School
Academic	Benjamin Graham

David LeFevre Dodd (August 23, 1895 – September 18, 1988) was an American educator, financial analyst, author, economist, professional investor, and in his student years, a protégé of, and as a postgraduate, close colleague of Benjamin Graham at Columbia Business School.

The Wall Street Crash of 1929 (Black Tuesday) almost wiped out Graham, who had started teaching the year before at his alma mater, Columbia. The crash inspired Graham to search for a more conservative, safer way to invest. Graham agreed to teach with the stipulation that someone take notes. Dodd, then a young instructor at Columbia, volunteered. Those transcriptions served as the basis for a 1934 book Security Analysis, which galvanized the concept of value investing. It is the longest running investment text ever published in 1934.

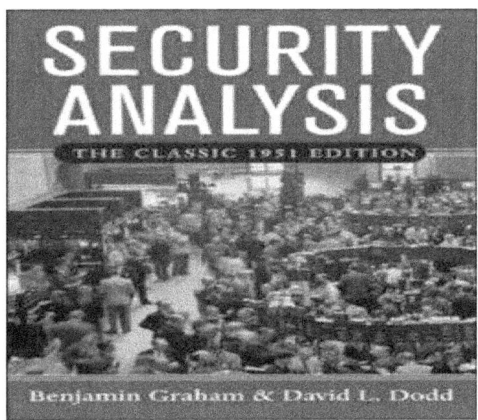

The phrases "Graham and Dodd," "*value investing*," "*margin of safety*," and "*intrinsic value*"—all biblical to value investors are often used interchangeably when referring to an approach to investing. Despite the onset of **modern portfolio theory** (MPT) in the late 1950s—a theory that peaked throughout the 80s, gaining Nobel recognition in 1990 (co-laureates: Harry Markowitz, Merton Miller, William F. Sharpe)—Value Investing proved to be a formidable style that sharply defied MPT. The University of Chicago was at the center of MPT, while Columbia has been the Mecca for Value Investing for 7½ decades. Many cracks in MPT are now well established, whereas the basics behind Graham & Dodd's approach to Value Investing are as valid today as when they were first introduced.

Value Investors see securities as either priced correctly, under-priced, or over-priced. In contrast, MPT proponents insist that, by definition under the efficient-market hypothesis, a realized price of a stock is the correct price. Value investor purists reject the usefulness of capital asset pricing model (CAPM), in part, because it wrongly extrapolates historical volatility as a proxy for risk. For example, if equity prices of a company fell 75%, assuming the underlying fundamentals of the company were solid, an MPT practitioner would view it as volatile (risky); whereas, a value investor would determine whether it was undervalued, and if so, buy it, reasoning that the resulting downward risk is less than before. Therefore, value investors see MPT metrics—such as standard deviation, beta (relative standard deviation), alpha (excess return), and the Sharpe ratio (risk adjusted return)—as inadequate and even misleading.

Columbia resisted de-emphasizing Value Investing during the throes of the MPT renaissance, but the appeal of MPT seemed to be part of a larger movement, thrusting finance aspects of business education into higher echelons of academia. During about a 25-year period (1965–90), published research and articles in leading journals of the value walk were few. Warren Buffett once commented, "You couldn't advance in a finance department in this country unless you taught that the world was flat." Shortly after the death of David Dodd in 1988, Bruce Greenwald, a star professor at CBS, took a keen interest in Value Investing. He found the overwhelming success of Value investors difficult to dismiss. At the same time, reliable data that fortified Value Investing was solidifying, while MPT was showing some flaws. Professor Greenwald invigorated the academic aspects of what many in ivory towers erstwhile treated as a vocational discipline.

MPT pundits argue that the Warren Buffett's long-term record is a statistical three- to five-sigma event—that is, his success is probable, but not replicable with certainty.

Yet the success of numerous other investment funds and practitioners who applied value investing theories weakened assertions attributing success to chance. Because Value Investing rejects MPT and its use of sophisticated statistics, there's irony when MPT theorists attribute its success to tails of standard deviation. Bruce Greenwald overhauled and relaunched the Value Investing curriculum at Columbia in the spring of 1994. Today, Value Investing enjoys broad appeal among academicians and investors around the world. Professor Greenwald is the Robert Heilbrunn Professor of Finance and Asset Management at Columbia University's Graduate School of Business.

3

Bruce Greenward

There are no bad days in the market. When the market is down, you've got bargains, and it's lovely to think of what you are buying at low prices. When the market is up, the bargains have gone, but you're rich.

Bruce Greenwald

Buce Corman Norbert Greenwald (born August 15, 1946), is a professor at Columbia University's Graduate School of Business and an advisor at First Eagle Investment Management. He is, among others, the author of the books Value Investing: from Graham to Buffett and beyond and Competition Demystified: A Radically Simplified Approach to Business Strategy. He has been referred to by The New York Times as "a guru to Wall Street's gurus" and is a recognized authority on value investing, along with additional expertise in productivity and the economics of information.

Greenwald has been recognized for his outstanding teaching abilities. He has been the recipient of numerous awards, including the Columbia University Presidential Teaching Award which honors the best of Columbia's teachers for maintaining the University's longstanding reputation for educational excellence. His classes are consistently oversubscribed, with more than 650 students taking his courses every year in subjects such as Value Investing, Economics of Strategic Behavior, Globalization of Markets, and Strategic Management of Media.

4
Warren Buffett

Born	Warren Edward Buffett August 30, 1930 (age 89) Omaha, Nebraska, U.S.
Education	University of Pennsylvania University of Nebraska–Lincoln (BS) Columbia University (MS)
Occupation	Businessman, investor, philanthropist
Years active	1951–present
Known for	Leadership of Berkshire Hathaway with Charlie Munger
Net worth	US$70.5 billion[1] (April 2020)

"If you don't believe in Value Investing, what do you believe in?"

Warren Buffett

Warren Edward Buffett born August 30, 1930 is an American business magnate, investor, and philanthropist, who is the chairman and CEO of Berkshire Hathaway. He is considered one of the most successful investors in the world and has a net worth of US$88.9 billion as of December 2019, making him the fourth-wealthiest person in the world.

Buffett was born in Omaha, Nebraska. He developed an interest in business and investing in his youth, eventually entering the Wharton School of the University of Pennsylvania in 1947 before transferring and graduating from the University of Nebraska at the age of 19. He went on to graduate from Columbia Business School, where he molded his investment philosophy around the concept of value investing that was pioneered by Benjamin Graham.

"The basic ideas of investing are to look at stocks as business, use the market's fluctuations to your advantage, and seek a margin of safety. That's what Ben Graham taught us. A hundred years from now they will still be the cornerstones of investing."

Warren Buffett

The value of businesses, irrespective of their current quoted price. He criticizes investment advisers who waste their time making forecasts about the economy, when it is much more important is to find good businesses that will remain good for years to come.

He also dismisses efficient market theory (EMT), which holds that there is no point analyzing and calculating the value of a business because the stock market, working with perfect efficiency, always reveals a company's value through its share price. In fact, he believes, prices only reflect value most of the time, and having total faith in them prevents people from actually trying to understand businesses. Buffett quotes his mentor, Ben Graham: "In the short run, the market is a voting machine but in the long run it is a weighing machine."

Stock market prices for companies are driven by emotion, not truth, and the truth about a company lies in its operating results rather than its current stock price or its glossy forecasts. Berkshire often makes its best acquisitions when fear is at its highest or sentiment about the market at its lowest. For the investor in fundamentals, these are times to buy; from 1965 to 2019 his return is 20.3%.

Berkshire's Performance vs. the S&P 500

Year	Annual Percentage Change in Per-Share Market Value of Berkshire	Annual Percentage Change in S&P 500 with Dividends Included
1965	49.5	10.0
1966	(3.4)	(11.7)
1967	13.3	30.9
1968	77.8	11.0
1969	19.4	(8.4)
1970	(4.6)	3.9
1971	80.5	14.6
1972	8.1	18.9
1973	(2.5)	(14.8)
1974	(48.7)	(26.4)
1975	2.5	37.2
1976	129.3	23.6
1977	46.8	(7.4)
1978	14.5	6.4
1979	102.5	18.2
1980	32.8	32.3
1981	31.8	(5.0)
1982	38.4	21.4
1983	69.0	22.4
1984	(2.7)	6.1
1985	93.7	31.6
1986	14.2	18.6
1987	4.6	5.1
1988	59.3	16.6
1989	84.6	31.7
1990	(23.1)	(3.1)
1991	35.6	30.5
1992	29.8	7.6
1993	38.9	10.1
1994	25.0	1.3
1995	57.4	37.6
1996	6.2	23.0
1997	34.9	33.4
1998	52.2	28.6
1999	(19.9)	21.0
2000	26.6	(9.1)
2001	6.5	(11.9)
2002	(3.8)	(22.1)
2003	15.8	28.7
2004	4.3	10.9
2005	0.8	4.9
2006	24.1	15.8
2007	28.7	5.5
2008	(31.8)	(37.0)
2009	2.7	26.5
2010	21.4	15.1
2011	(4.7)	2.1
2012	16.8	16.0
2013	32.7	32.4
2014	27.0	13.7
2015	(12.5)	1.4
2016	23.4	12.0
2017	21.9	21.8
2018	2.8	(4.4)
2019	11.0	31.5
Compounded Annual Gain – 1965-2019	20.3%	10.0%
Overall Gain – 1964-2019	2,744,062%	19,784%

Buffett famously does not invest in industries he does not fully understand. He was widely criticized for entering the technology stocks boom of the late 1990s, instead buying companies that produced boring things like paint, bricks and carpets. His golden rule is, invest only in your 'circle of competence' – areas you know something about, where you can understand how a company makes its money. A quote from Thomas Watson of IBM sums up Buffett's philosophy: *"I'm no genius. I'm smart in spots – but I stay around those spots."* Like everyone else, he appreciates the growth to the economy that new ideas and technologies bring, but as an investor, he notes, "…our reaction to a fermenting industry is much like our attitude toward space exploration: We applaud the endeavour but prefer to skip the ride."

- Invest only in a company whose business you understand.

- Invest only in companies whose earnings will surely be higher in the future than they are now.

- Look for companies that have a 'durable competitive advantage'. Even if their stock price goes up and down, this advantage will naturally see it outperform other stocks.

- When you do buy a stock, buy it for the long haul ("If you aren't willing to own a stock for ten years, don't even think about owning it for ten minutes.").

Buffett likes to invest in what he calls The Inevitable, companies whose products will still be bought 10, 20 30 years from now, and whose brand is so famous it gives them the lion's share of a market. Berkshire has had large holdings in Coca Cola and Gillette for many years because although things like distribution, manufacturing processes and product innovation will evolve, people will still be drinking Coke and needing to shave for our investment lifetimes, and they will turn to the trusted names.

His approach is if you find a small number of companies with a strong competitive advantage and at reasonable prices, why diversify? Paradoxically, putting more of your money into a smaller number of carefully chosen stocks means you can relax. In any given year, Berkshire Hathaway may make only a handful of investments in the stock market, sometimes none at all. Often, Buffett notes, the smartest investment move is inactivity:

"Charlie and I decided long ago that in an investment lifetime it's too hard to make hundreds of smart decisions...Therefore, we adopted a strategy that required our being smart – and not too smart at that – only a very few times. Indeed, we'll now settle for one good idea a year. (Charlie says it's my turn)."

Annual Report (1993)

Warren Buffett and close friend Katherine Graham, chairman of the Washington Post from 1973 to 1991.

According to Buffett's 1984 speech The Super investors of Graham-and-Doddsville, in 1973, Mr. Market was offering to sell the Post for $80 million. Buffett also mentioned that you could have "…sold the (Post's) assets to any one of ten buyers for not less than $400 million, probably appreciably more."

"I have never been able to figure out why it's riskier to buy $400 million worth of properties for $40 million than $80 million. And, as a matter of fact, if you buy a group of such securities and you know anything at all about business valuation, there is essentially no risk in buying $400 million for $80 million, particularly if you do it by buying ten $40 million piles of $8 million each." On margin of safety "You don't try and buy businesses worth $83 million for $80 million. You leave yourself an enormous margin. When you build a bridge, you insist it can carry 30,000 pounds, but you only drive 10,000 pound trucks across it. And that same principle works in investing."

5
Charlie Munger

Charlie Munger

Munger at Berkshire Hathaway's 2010 shareholder meeting

Born	Charles Thomas Munger January 1, 1924 (age 96) Omaha, Nebraska, U.S.
Alma mater	University of Michigan California Institute of Technology Harvard University (JD)
Occupation	Vice Chairman, Berkshire Hathaway
Known for	Leading investments at Berkshire Hathaway with Warren Buffett
Net worth	US$1.8 billion (Mar 2019)[1]

"All intelligent investing is value investing, acquiring more than you are paying for. You must value the business in order to value the stock."

Charles Thomas Munger (born January 1, 1924) is an American investor, businessman, former real estate attorney, and philanthropist. He is vice chairman of Berkshire Hathaway, the conglomerate controlled by Warren Buffett; Buffett has described Munger as his partner. Munger served as chairman of Wesco Financial Corporation from 1984 through 2011. He is also chairman of the Daily Journal Corporation, based in Los Angeles, California, and a director of Costco Wholesale Corporation.

He moved with his family to California, where he joined the law firm Wright & Garrett (later Musick, Peeler & Garrett). In 1962 he founded and worked as a real estate attorney at Munger, Tolles & Olson LLP. He then gave up the practice of law to concentrate on managing investments and later partnered with Otis Booth in real estate development. He then partnered with Jack Wheeler to form Wheeler, Munger, and Company, an investment firm with a seat on the Pacific Coast Stock Exchange. He wound up Wheeler, Munger, and Co. in 1976, after losses of 32% in 1973 and 31% in 1974.

Although Munger is better known for his association with Buffett, he ran an investment partnership of his own from 1962 to 1975. According to Buffett's essay, "The Superinvestors of Graham-and-Doddsville", published in 1984, Munger's investment partnership generated compound annual returns of 19.8% during the 1962–75 period compared to a 5.0% annual appreciation rate for the Dow.

In multiple speeches and in the book Poor Charlie's Almanack: The Wit and Wisdom of Charles T. Munger's worldly wisdom consists of a set of mental models framed as a latticework to help solve critical business problems. Munger uses the term "Lollapalooza effect" for multiple biases, tendencies or mental models acting in compound with each other at the same time in the same direction. With the Lollapalooza effect, itself a mental model, the result is often extreme, due to the confluence of the mental models, biases or tendencies acting together, greatly increasing the likelihood of acting irrationally.

"Basically, all investment is value investment in the sense that you're always trying to get better prospects that you're paying for. But you can't look everywhere at once. Just any more than you could run a marathon in 12 states at once. And so you have to have some system of thinking some place to look which is your hunting ground. But you're looking for value in every case...I think the strongest companies are not in America. I think Chinese companies are stronger than ours, growing faster... It really helps if

you know which hunting ground to look in. Where we all do better hunting and hunting where the hunting is easy. I have a friend who's a fisherman. He said I have a simple rule for success in fishing, "Fish where the fish are." You want to fish where the bargains are. It's that simple. If the fishing is really lousy where you are, look for another place to fish."

Munger and Buffett don't just buy any stock. They have a system in place, and they use it to evaluate whether or not a company is undervalued relative to the market. They're looking for a few gems that will provide outsized returns. Even in their portfolio, the vast majority of the profits come from a very small section.

Charlie Munger at USC Business School in 1994. The full title of the talk is ""A Lesson on Elementary, Worldly Wisdom as It Relates to Investment Management & Business".

You've got to have models in your head. And you've got to array your experience—both vicarious and direct—on this latticework of models. You may have noticed students who just try to remember and pound back what is remembered. Well, they fail in school and in life. You've got to hang experience on a latticework of models in your head.

What are the models? Well, the first rule is that you've got to have multiple models—because if you just have one or two that you're using, the nature of human psychology is such that you'll torture reality so that it fits your models, or at least you'll think it does

It's like the old saying, "To the man with only a hammer, every problem looks like a nail." And of course, that's the way the chiropractor goes about practicing medicine. But that's a perfectly disastrous way to think and a perfectly disastrous way to operate in the world. So you've got to have multiple models.

"How do some people get wiser than other people? Partly it is inborn temperament. Some people do not have a good temperament for investing. They're too fretful; they worry too much. But if you've got a good temperament, which **basically means being very patient, yet combine that with a vast aggression when you know enough to do something, then you just gradually learn the game, partly by doing, partly by studying. Obviously, the more hard lessons you can learn vicariously, instead of from your own terrible experiences, the better off you will be. I don't know anyone who did it with great rapidity. Warren Buffett has become one hell of a lot better investor since the day I met him and so have I. If we had been frozen at any given stage, with the knowledge hand** we had, the record would have been much worse than it is. So the game is to keep learning, and I don't think people are going to keep learning who don't like the learning process."

"Beta and modern portfolio theory and the like – none of it makes any sense to me. We're trying to buy businesses with sustainable competitive advantages at a low, or even a fair, price."

"I was in New York City with Charlie to attend a Salomon Brother's board meeting. We had come out of the building and were standing on the sidewalk, discussing what had transpired at the meeting. At least, that's what I thought we were doing, for suddenly I realized that I had been talking to myself for some time. I looked around for Charlie, only to see him climbing into the back of a taxicab, headed off to the airport. No goodbye, no nothing.

People think it's Charlie's eyes that cause him to miss seeing things (Charlie lost his vision in one eye many years ago due to complications from cataract surgery). BUT IT'S NOT HIS EYES, IT'S HIS HEAD! I once sat through three sets of traffic lights, and plenty of honking behind us, as Charlie discussed some complex problem at an intersection."

"I would say everything about Charlie is unusual. I've been looking for the usual now for forty years, and I have yet to find it. Charlie marches to his own music and its music like virtually no one else is listening to. So, I would say that to try and typecast Charlie in terms of any other human that I can think of, no one would fit. He's got his own mold." –

Warren & Charlie

The Psychology of Human Misjudgement, by Charlie Munger.

Causes of Human Misjudgement

1.   Under recognition of the power of what psychologists call reinforcement and economists call incentives.

One of my favourite cases about the power of incentives is the Federal Express case. The heart and soul of the integrity of the system is that all the packages have to be shifted rapidly in one central location each night. And the system has no integrity if the whole shift can't be done fast. And Federal Express had one hell of a time getting the thing to work. And they tried moral suasion, they tried everything in the world, and finally, somebody got the happy thought that they were paying the night shift by the hour and that maybe if they paid them by the shift, the system would work better. And behold, that solution worked.

Early in the history of Xerox, Joe Wilson, who was then in the government, had to go back to Xerox because he couldn't understand how their better, new machine was selling so poorly in relation to their older and inferior machine. Of course, when he got there, he found out that the commission arrangement with the salesmen gave a tremendous incentive to the inferior machine.

2.   *Simple psychological denial.*

This first really hit me between the eyes when a friend of our family had a super-athlete, super-student son who flew off a carrier in the north Atlantic and never came back, and his mother, who was a very sane woman, just never believed that he was dead. And, of course, if you turn on the television, you find the mothers of the most obvious criminals that man could ever diagnose, and they all think their sons are innocent. That's simple psychological denial. The reality is too painful to bear, so you just distort it until it's bearable. We all do that to some extent, and it's a common psychological misjudgement that causes terrible problems.

3.   *Incentive-cause bias.*

Both in one's own mind and that of one's trusted advisor, where it creates what economists call agency costs. Here, my early experience was a doctor who sent bushel baskets full of normal gallbladders down to the pathology lab in the leading hospital in Lincoln,

Nebraska. And with that quality control for which community hospitals are famous, about five years after he should've been removed from the staff, he was.

And one of the old doctors who participated in the removal was also a family friend, and I asked him, I said, "Tell me, did he think, here's a way for me to exercise my talents," this guy was very skilled technically, "And make a high living by doing a few maimings and murders every year, along with some frauds?" And he said, "Hell no, Charlie. He thought that the gallbladder was the source of all medical evil, and if you really love your patients, you couldn't get that organ out rapidly enough.

4.   Superpower in error-causing psychological tendency, bias from consistency and commitment tendency, including the tendency to avoid or promptly resolve cognitive dissonance.

Includes the self-confirmation tendency of all conclusions, particularly expressed conclusions, and with a special persistence for conclusions that are hard-won.

Well, what I'm saying here is that the human mind is a lot like the human egg, and the human egg has a shut-off device. When one sperm gets in, it shuts down so the next one can't get in. The human mind has a big tendency of the same sort. And here again, it doesn't just catch ordinary mortals, it catches the deans of physics. According to Max Planck, the really innovative, important new physics was never really accepted by the old guard.

5. Bias from Pavlovian association, misconstruing past correlation as a reliable basis for decision-making.

Practically, I'd say 3/4 of advertising works on pure Pavlov. Think how association, pure association, works. Take Coca-Cola Company we're the biggest share-holder. They want to be associated with every wonderful image, heroics in the Olympics, wonderful music, you name it. They don't want to be associated with Presidents' funerals and so forth. When have you seen a Coca-Cola ad, and the association really works.

6. Bias from reciprocation tendency, including the tendency of one on a roll to act as other persons expect.

Well here, again, Cialdini does a magnificent job at this, and you're all going to be given a copy of Cialdini's book. And if you have half as much sense as I think you do, you will immediately order copies for all of your children and several of your friends. You will never make a better investment.

It is so easy to be a patsy for what he calls the compliance practitioners of this life. But, at any rate, reciprocation tendency is a very, very powerful phenomenon, and Cialdini demonstrated this by running around campus, and he asked people to take juvenile delinquents to the zoo. And it was a campus, and so one in six actually agreed to do it. And after he'd accumulated a statistical output he went around on the same campus and he asked other people, he said, "Gee, would you devote two afternoons a week to taking juvenile delinquents somewhere and suffering greatly yourself to help them," and there he got 100% of the people to say no.

But after he'd made the first request, he backed off a little, and he said, "Would you at least take them to the zoo one afternoon?" He raised the compliance rate from a third to a half. He got three times the success by just going through the little ask-for-a-lot-and-back-off.

Now if the human mind, on a subconscious level, can be manipulated that way and you don't know it, I always use the phrase, "You're like a one-legged man in an ass-kicking contest." I mean you are really giving a lot of quarter to the external world that you can't afford to give, and on this so-called role theory, where you tend to act in the way that other people expect, and that's reciprocation if you think about the way society is organized.

7. His is a lollapalooza, and Henry Kaufman wisely talked about this, bias from over-influence by social proof, that is, the conclusions of others, particularly under conditions of natural uncertainty and stress.

And here, one of the cases the psychologists use is Kitty Genovese, where all these people, I don't know, 50, 60, 70 of them just sort of sat and did nothing while she was slowly murdered. Now one of the explanations is that everybody looked at everybody else and nobody else was doing anything, and so there's automatic social proof that the right thing to do is nothing.

Big-shot businessmen get into these waves of social proof. Do you remember some years ago when one Oil Company bought a fertilizer company, and every other major oil company practically ran out and bought a fertilizer company? And there was no more damned reason for all these oil companies to buy fertilizer companies, but they didn't know exactly what to do, and if Exxon was doing it, it was good enough for Mobil, and vice versa. I think they're all gone now, but it was a total disaster.

8. Bias from contrast caused distortions of sensation, perception, and cognition.

Here the great experiment that Cialdini does in his class is he takes three buckets of water. One's hot, one's cold, and one's room temperature. And he has the student stick his left hand in the hot water and his right hand in the cold water. Then he has them remove the hands and put them both in the room temperature bucket, and of course with both hands in the same bucket of water, one seems hot, and the other seems cold because the sensation apparatus of man is over-influenced by contrast. It has no absolute scale. It's got a contrast scale in it, and it's scale with quantum effects in it, too. It takes a certain percentage change before it's noticed.

Maybe you've had a magician remove your watch; I certainly have, without your noticing it. It's the same thing. He's taking advantage of your contrast type troubles and your sensory apparatus. But here the great truth is that cognition mimic's sensation, and the cognition manipulators mimic the watch-removing magician. In other words, people are manipulating you all day long on this contrast phenomenon.

9.   Bias from over-influence by authority.

Over-influence by authority has another very … you'll like this one. You got a pilot and a co-pilot. The pilot is the authority figure. They don't do this in airplanes, but they've done it in simulators. They have the pilot do something where the co-pilot who's been trained in simulators a long time. He knows he's not to allow the plane to crash. They have the pilot to do something where an idiot co-pilot would know the plane was going to crash, but the pilot's doing it, and the co-pilot is sitting there, and the pilot is the authority figure. 25% of the time, the plane crashes. This is a very powerful psychological tendency.

10.   Bias from Deprival Super Reaction Syndrome, including bias caused by present or threatened scarcity, including threatened removal of something almost possessed but never possessed. Here I took the Munger dog, a lovely harmless dog.

The only way to get that dog to bite you was to try and take something out of its mouth after it was already there.

The extreme business coke here was New Coke. Now Coca-Cola has the most valuable trademark in the world. We're the major shareholder. I think we understand that trademark. Coke has armies of brilliant engineers, lawyers, psychologists, advertising executives, and so forth. And they had a trademark on a flavor, and they'd spent better part of 100 years getting people to believe that trademark had all these intangible values, too. And people associate it with a flavor, so they were going to tell people not that it was improved 'cause you can't improve a flavor. If a flavor's a matter of taste, you may improve a detergent or something, but telling you're going to make a major change in a flavor, I mean … So they got this huge Deprival Super Reaction Syndrome.

11.   Bias from envy/jealousy.

 Well, envy/jealousy made what, two out of the 10 commandments. Those of you who've raised siblings or tried to run a law firm or investment bank or even a faculty. I've heard Warren say a half a dozen times, "It's not greed that drives the world but envy."

Here again, you go through the psychology survey courses. You go to the index: envy, jealousy. In a thousand-page book, it's blank! There are some blind spots in academia. But it's an enormously powerful thing, and it operates to a considerable extent at a subconscious level, and anybody who doesn't understand it is taking on defects he shouldn't have.

12. Bias from chemical dependency

Well, we don't have to talk about that. We've all seen so much of it, but it's interesting how it always causes moral breakdown if there's any need, and it always involves massive denial. It aggravates what we talked about earlier in the aviator case, the tendency to distort reality so that it's endurable.

13. Bias from gambling compulsion.

The truth of the matter is the devisers of these modern machines and techniques know a lot of things that Skinner didn't know. For instance, a lottery ... you have a lottery where you get your number by lot and then somebody draws a number by lot? It gets lousy play. You get a lottery where people get to pick their number, get big play. Again, it's this consistency and commitment thing. People think that if they've committed to it, it has to be good. The minute they've picked it themselves, it gets an extra validity. After all, they thought it and they acted on it.

Then if you take slot machines, you get bar, bar, lemon. It happens again and again and again. You get all these near misses. Well, that's Deprival Super Reaction Syndrome, and boy do the people who create the machines understand human psychology.

14.   Bias from liking distortion, including the tendency to especially like oneself, one's own kind, and one's own idea structures, and the tendency to be especially susceptible to being misled by someone liked.

The guy tells you what is good for him, and he doesn't recognize that he's doing anything wrong any more than that doctor did when he was pulling out all those normal gallbladders. He believed that his own idea structures will cure cancer, and he believed that the demons that he's the guardian against are the biggest demons and the most important ones. And in fact, they may be very small demons compared to the demons that you face. So you're getting your advice in this world from your paid advisor with this huge load of ghastly bias. And woe to you!

15.   Bias from the non-mathematical nature of the human brain in its natural state as it deals with probabilities employing crude heuristics and is often mislead by mere contrast.

The tendency to overweigh conveniently available information and other psychological rooted mis-thinking tendencies on this list when the brain should be using the simple probability mathematics of Fermat and Pascal, applied to all reasonably attainable and correctly weighted items of information that are of value in predicting outcomes.

The right way to think is the way Zeckhauser plays Bridge. It's just that simple.

And your brain doesn't naturally know how to think the way Zeckhauser knows to play Bridge. Now you notice I put in that availability thing, and there I'm mimicking some very eminent psychologists … Tversky, who raised the idea of availability to a whole heuristic of misjudgment.

You know, they are very substantially right. Ask the Coca-Cola Company, which has raised availability to a secular religion, if availability changes behavior. You'll drink a hell of a lot more Coke if it's always available. Availability does change behavior and cognition.

16. Bias from over-influence by extra vivid evidence.

Here's one … I'm at least $30 million poorer as I sit here giving this little talk because I once bought 300 shares of a stock, and the guy called me back and said, "I got 1500 more." I said, "Will you hold it for 15 minutes while I think about it?" In CEO of this company, I've seen a lot of vivid peculiarities in a long life, but this guy set a world record. I'm talking about the CEO, and I just mis-weighed it. The truth of the matter is his situation was foolproof. He was soon gonna be dead. I turned down the extra 1500 share, and it's now cost me $30 million, and that's life in the big city.

17. Stress-induced mental changes, small and large, temporary and permanent.

Other normal limitations of sensation, memory, cognition and knowledge. Well, I don't have time for that. Stress-induced mental changes. Here, my favourite example is the great Pavlov. He had all these dogs in cages, which had all been conditioned into changed behaviors, and the great Leningrad flood came, and it just went right up. The dog's in a cage, and the dog had as much stress as you can imagine a dog ever having. The water receded in time to save some of the dogs, and Pavlov noted that they'd had a total reversal of their conditioned personality. Well, being the great scientist he was, he spent the rest of his life giving nervous breakdowns to dogs, and he learned a hell of a lot that I regard as very interesting. I have never known any Freudian analyst who knew anything about the last work of Pavlov, and I never met a lawyer who understood that what Pavlov found out with those dogs had anything to do with programming, and de-programming, and cults and so forth.

Introduction to Value Investing

"Value investing is the discipline of buying securities at a significant discount from their current underlying values and holding them until more of their value is realized. The element of a bargain is the key to the process."

– Seth Klarman, *Margin of Safety*

6

Value Investing

Value investing is an investment strategy that involves picking stocks that appear to be trading for less than their intrinsic or book value. They believe the market overreacts to good and bad news, resulting in stock price movements that do not correspond to a company's long-term fundamentals.

What is mean by name value investing?

- **Value** – the word value derived by the sense to value of company or business, business can be value in different ways, we see use asset-based valuation which was founded by Benjamin Graham and David Dodd in 1934. when we value a business, we see underpriced value by some form of fundamental analysis.
  Value also mean Intrinsic value refers to an investor's perception of the inherent value of an asset, such as a company, stock, option, or real estate. Knowing an investment's intrinsic value is useful for value investors who have a goal of buying stocks and other investments at

a discount to this amount. In this book we will learn, how to find intrinsic value by using assets value and other valuation approach. The goal of value investing is to seek out stocks that are trading for less than their intrinsic value.

- **Investing** -To invest is to allocate money in the expectation of some benefit in the future, for value investor , we first understand the company in details then we invest to gain high return from our investment .In investing three principal is important to keep in mind , one is amount we are investing , second is the return we are expecting and third is the time horizon , there three principal are very important in investing , as a value investor one need to be willing to invest his money for long term so that we can able to generate good return and with no risk .

Value investing is a Discipline process to measure the value of underlying of financial securities. Value investing is also known as the fundamental valuation of a company to buy bargain stock.

There are different Approaches of Investing

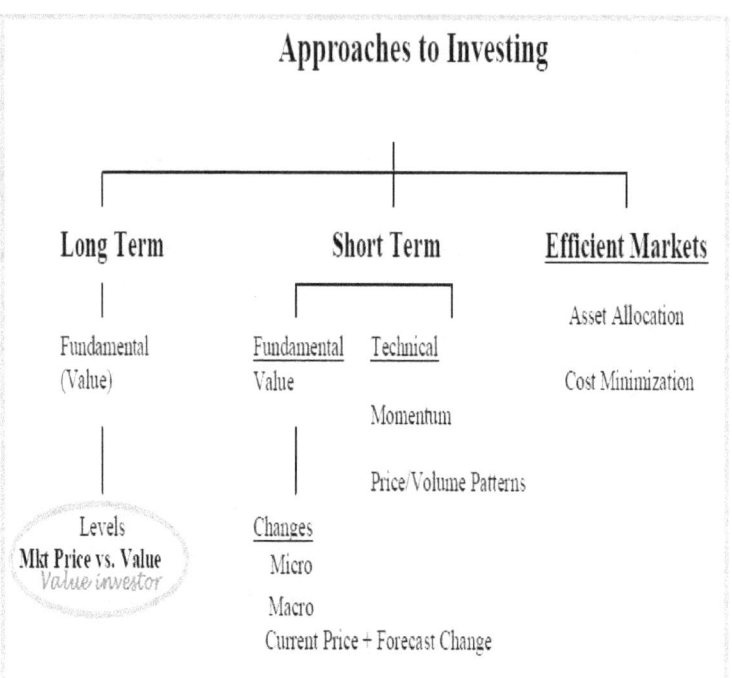

You can see there are different branches of approaches, each represent different approach of investing.

- **Long Team Approach -** You can approach long-term investing by determining the rate of return you want, then looking for averages rate of return over a five to 10-year period. When you invest for the long-term you must not panic when a stock's value drops and avoid selling just because the market looks bad.

In Long term approach we will go through the fundamental value approach, in fundamental value approach we will go through the which industry company operate in, position in the industry, market share, business have competitive advantage , we will also see the different approaches of valuation like assets value , earning power value and franchise value and once will done with the valuation approach , we will move further to intrinsic value to market value , we will also see what margin of safety we have before we invest in the company .

- **Short Term Approach -** Investing isn't typically a get rich quick tactic that you can do for a short period of time and expect to make a significant amount of money, while many people like to play the market or speculate with day trading, it's a risky business and you should educate yourself and do plenty of research before you try short-term investing. Short-term investments are usually sold after holding them for three years or less. In this approach analyst forecast for quarterly or early basis. Generally analyst forecast the earning of the company, if the earning meet the target they make profit or they may born for huge losses. Analyst mainly see stock goes up and down .They check the current price and forecast changes as per the earning and other factors .

- **Fundamental Value** – Analyst forecast the earning based on fundamental value of the business both in micro and macro level to gain short term profit due to the fluctuation in the share price.

- **Technical / Quantities** –Analyst look at the trading pattern of chart and volume. Analyst check the momentum for their approach of investing. They project short term price projection based on the patterns .They even buy when the price is going upward trend. Analysts even look for company interest rate for and try to forecast the price.

- **Efficient Market** - Market efficiency refers to the degree to which market prices reflect all available, relevant information. If markets are efficient, then all information is already incorporated into prices, and so there is no way to "beat" the market because there are no undervalued or overvalued securities available. Note that this thought experiment does not necessarily imply that stock prices are unpredictable. For example, suppose that the piece of information in question says that a financial crisis is likely to come soon. Investors typically do not like to hold stocks during a financial crisis, and thus investors may sell stocks until the price drops enough so that the expected return compensates for this risk. EMH does not require that investors be rational; it says that individual investors will act randomly, but as a whole, the market is always "right." In simple terms, "efficient" implies "normal." For example, an unusual reaction to unusual information is normal. If a crowd suddenly starts running in one direction, it's normal for you to run in that direction as well, even if there isn't a rational reason for doing so.

The Three Principal of Value Investing

- **Mr. Market**
- **Value & Price**
- **Margin of Safety & Circle of Competence.**

Mr. Market - Graham asks the reader to imagine that he is one of the two owners of a business, along with a partner called Mr. Market. The partner frequently offers to sell his share of the business or to buy the reader's share. This partner is what today would be called manic-depressive, with his estimate of the business's value going from very pessimistic to wildly optimistic. The reader is always free to decline the partner's offer, since he will soon come back with an entirely different offer.

Mr. Market is often identified as having human behavioral manic depressive characteristics as follows:

1. Is emotional, euphoric, moody.
2. Is often irrational.
3. Offers those transactions are strictly at your option.
4. Is there to serve you, not to guide you.
5. Is in the short run a voting machine, in the long run a weighing machine.
6. Will offer you a chance to buy low, and sell high.

7. Is frequently efficient…but not always.

This behavior of Mr. Market allows the investor to wait until Mr. Market is in a 'pessimistic mood' and offers low sale price. The investor has the option to buy at that low price. Therefore, patience is an important virtue when dealing with Mr. Market.

Graham, and the students that follow him, believe that investors are better off assessing the value of stocks through fundamental analysis, and then deciding whether the future prospects of a company warrant a purchase or sale of the security.

Since Mr. Market is so emotional, it will offer up opportunities for diligent investors to enter and exit at favorable times. When Mr. Market gets too pessimistic, valuations on good stocks will be favorable allowing investors to purchase them at a reasonable price relative to their future potential. When Mr. Market is overly optimistic this may provide a good time to sell the stock at a valuation which is unjustified.

Value & Price – value investors see stocks as a part of a business. They do not base their investment decisions on historic price movements like traders do, but instead they try to determine what that small part of business is worth and invest only when they can buy it for a price lower than that value. In short, value investors try to buy a dollar of value at a price of fifty cents. Exploiting differences between price and value is the cornerstone of value investing.

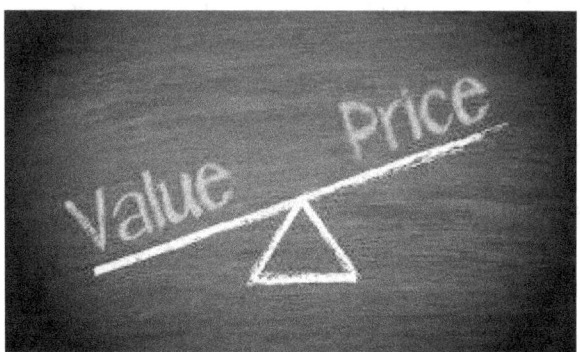

"In the short-run, the market is a voting machine - reflecting a voter-registration test that requires only money, not intelligence or emotional stability - but in the long-run, the market is a weighing machine."

Warren Buffett in Letter to Berkshire Shareholders (1993)

There is a significant difference between intrinsic value and market value, though both are ways of value a company. Intrinsic value is an estimate of the actual true value of a company, regardless of market value. Market value is the current value of a company as reflected by the company's stock price. Therefore, market value may be significantly higher or lower than the intrinsic value. Market value is also commonly used to refer to the market capitalization of a publicly-traded company and is obtained by multiplying the number of its outstanding shares by the current share price.

The market value is usually higher than the intrinsic value if there is strong investment demand, leading to possible overvaluation. The opposite is true if there is weak investment demand, which can result in the undervaluation of the company.

Margin of Safety & Circle of Competence. *-* Margin of safety is a principle of investing in which an investor only purchases securities when their market price is significantly below their intrinsic value. In other words, when the market price of a security is significantly below your estimation of its intrinsic value, the difference is the margin of safety. Because investors may set a margin of safety in accordance with their own risk preferences, buying securities when this difference is present allows an investment to be made with minimal downside risk.

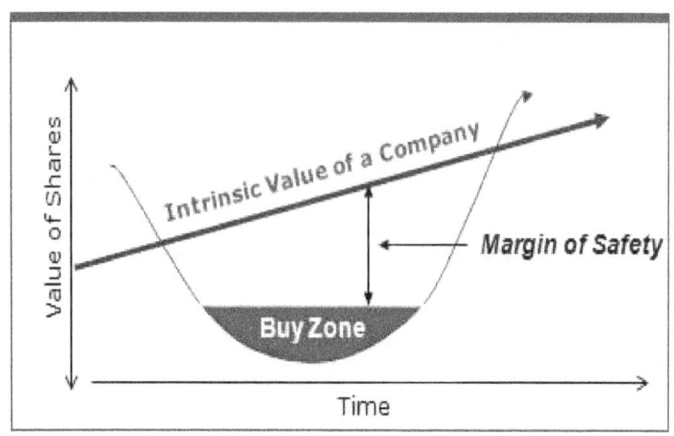

As scholarly as Graham was, his principle was based on simple truths. He knew that a stock priced at $1 today could just as likely be valued at 50 cents or $1.50 in the future. He also recognized that the current valuation of $1 could be off, which means he would be subjecting himself to unnecessary risk. He concluded that if he could buy a stock at a discount to its intrinsic value, he would limit his losses substantially. Although there was no guarantee that the stock's price would increase, the discount provided the margin of safety he needed to ensure that his losses would be minimal.

"When you build a bridge, you insist it can carry 30,000 pounds, but you only drive 10,000-pound trucks across it. And that same principle works in investing."

Using margin of safety, one should buy a stock when it is worth more than its price in the market. This is the central thesis of value investing philosophy which espouses preservation of capital as its first rule of investing.

A circle of competence is the subject area which matches a person's skills or expertise. The mental model was developed by Warren Buffett and Charlie Munger to describe limiting one's financial investments in areas where an individual may have limited understanding or experience, concentrating in areas where one has the greatest familiarity, and to emphasize the importance of aligning a subjective assessment of one owns competence with actual competence. Buffett summarized the concept in the motto, "Know your circle of competence, and stick within it. The size of that circle is not very important; knowing its boundaries, however, is vital.

The concept of the Circle of Competence has been used over the years by Warren Buffett as a way to focus investors on only operating in areas they knew best. The bones of the concept appear in his 1996 Shareholder Letter:

What an investor needs is the ability to correctly evaluate selected businesses. Note that word "selected": You don't have to be an expert on every company, or even many. You only have to be able to evaluate companies within your circle of competence. The size of that circle is not very important; knowing its boundaries, however, is vital.

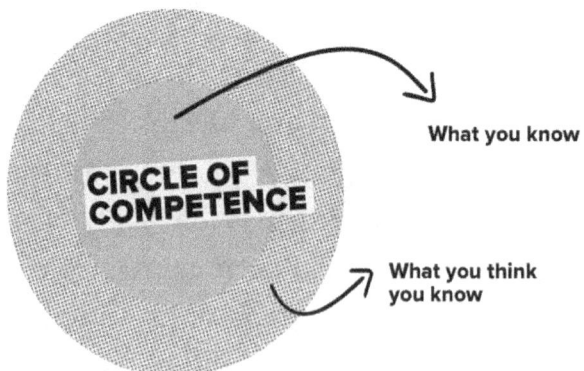

"I'm no genius. I'm smart in spots—but I stay around those spots."

Tom Watson Sr., Founder of IBM

Buffett describes the circle of competence of one of his business managers, a Russian immigrant with poor English who built the largest furniture store in Nebraska:

I couldn't have given her $200 million worth of Berkshire Hathaway stock when I bought the business because she doesn't understand stock. She understands cash. She understands furniture. She understands real estate. She doesn't understand stocks, so she doesn't have anything to do with them. If you deal with Mrs. B in what I would call her circle of competence... She is going to buy 5,000 end tables this afternoon (if the price is right). She is going to buy 20 different carpets in odd lots and everything else like that because she understands carpet. She wouldn't buy 100 shares of General Motors if it was at 50 cents a share.

The first principal we understood is the Mr. Market as sometime stock price not represent to their actual value of the business , second is that every securities have fundamental values to Price, we need to study depth of the company fundamental valuation to know the intrinsic value compare to the price available in the market then we can estimate the margin of safety and pay below the price and have enough margin of safety around 30% and most important the business should be within your circle of competence. There should not be any area of risk involve.

Value investors analyse the value of those securities and then compare it to the price that is quoted by Mr. Market and then find do they have enough of a margin of safety and if the security is trading at a sufficiently low value compared to that fundamental value, you take a position and invest.

Reason to be a Value investor

First are the markets being not efficient, value investor takes advantage of the market due to this performance high compare to growth investing, as we see warren buffett performance 20% above CAGR for more than 50 years.

- **High Margin of Safety-** A value investor purchases stocks that are trading at a significant discount to their intrinsic value. This difference between the intrinsic value and the purchase price is known as the margin of safety.

- **Low-Risk Portfolio** - With a smaller, low-risk portfolio of value stocks, you can focus on the indicators related to just a few stocks. Aside from minimizing the risk of losing a lot of money in a short period of time, this will also improve your efficiency as a trader.

- **Small Losses, Massive Returns** - Value stocks are purchased when they are trading below their intrinsic value. The trader has the option of selling the stock at a time when it is trading at or above its actual value. Undervalued stocks have a potential for generating exponential profits over time if they can successfully turn around.

Control over Holdings- Value investing is a safe option for investors as it allows them control over individual holdings. If you dislike a particular company due to moral or personal reasons, you can remove your money from the company without exiting the fund.

How to be a Good Value investor

- Understand your strength and weakness and use your knowledge to grow your investment.

- Use the knowledge you have in the industry – to know what you know then what you don't know.

- To know what you are expert in, use your expertise in investing, and always know your edge in investing and selecting the company.

- Discover the area you know so well; it can be a product you understand.

	Berkshire Hathaway	S&P 500	Annual Outperformance
1960s	28.3%	5.0%	23.3%
1970s	22.2%	5.9%	16.3%
1980s	39.1%	17.3%	21.7%
1990s	20.5%	18.0%	2.5%
2000s	5.9%	-1.0%	6.8%
2010s	17.9%	15.3%	2.6%
1965-2014	21.7%	9.8%	11.8%

As you can learn from the famous investor like Warren Buffett and Charlie Munger, their performance in Berkshire Hathaway.

What Requires to a Good Value Investor

If you find , there are very few value investor , it might sound strange but it true , nobody want to be slow to make money , today world everyone want to be super rich in short period of time and it never happens !. Value investing is essentially psychologically unnatural.

- Value investor invest when other are not investing ,when market have a negative trend and investor have Herd Mentality Bias , they are tendency to follow and copy what other investors are doing and at time you are investing and buying at bargain price with enough margin of safety .

- Humility & Patience is the virtue to be successful value investor weapons, when there is bad news in the financial market at that time value investor need to very much humility and have lots of patience, there is no need to take any action, just wait for the right time to invest.

- When value investor don't find any bargain price stock due to any reason, like market is in high trend, he should be doing nothing.

- Value investor should be holding his portfolio for long period of time for the high return.

- Keep enough cash to invest when the right time comes as example of warren buffett, he is always holding around $100 Billion and wait for the right time to invest.

- Value investor must have discipline approach of investing, he should be know the value investing process and should not divert from the principal.

How to be a successful Value investor

There are two ways to be successful value Investor.

First way

- Why is this opportunity available only to me?
- Why I am only one seeing this opportunity?
- What is the other side of transition coming from?
- What the other side know that I don't know?
- What is the opposite view?
- Why the other is selling and I am buying?

This is call adverse selection a market situation where buyers and sellers have different information, so that a participant might participate selectively in trades which benefit them the most, at the expense of the other trader.

Buyers sometimes have better information about how much benefit they can extract from a service. For example, an all-you-can-eat buffet restaurant that sets one price for all customers risks being adversely selected against by high appetite and hence, the least profitable customers. The restaurant has no way of knowing whether a given customer has a high or low appetite. The customer is the only one who knows if they have a high or low appetite. In this case the high appetite customers are more likely to use the information they have and to go to the restaurant.

The second way to be a successful investor must have three attributes: -

- Character determines your return, how you behave in the market.

- Temperament needs to be control, should not flow with the market.

- Ability to stay in the market for long term , because investor have a behavioral biases, they sell the winners stocks and hold the losers stocks.

7
The Process of Value Investing

- *Search Good Stock*
- *Valuation*
- *Strategic Analysis*
- *Risk & Safety*

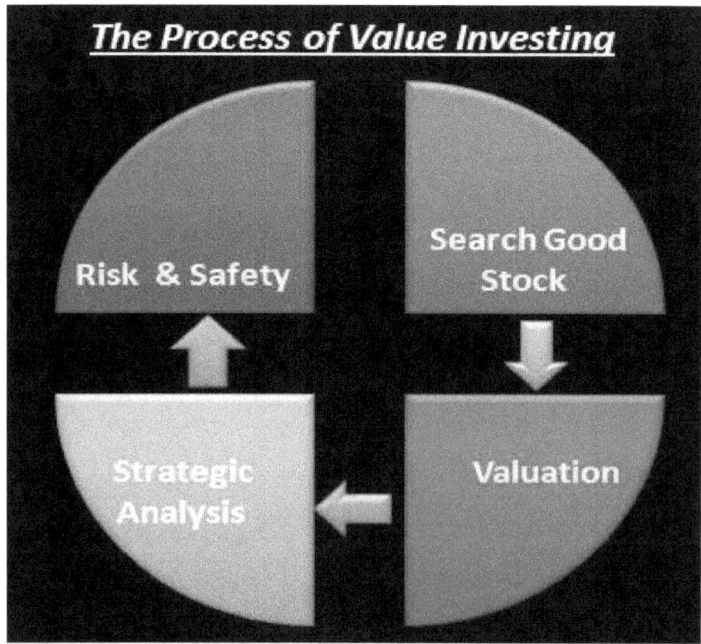

Search Good Stock

There are thousand and millions of securities investment idea available and we will not look for all, so there we need to look for a search of good stock, which have deep moat around it and must be consumer type company, value investor look search for a company within the circle of Competence, finding right stock to search will make sure that you are in the right side of the trade, your valuation side approach should be better than the other side of the trade, to do focus investigation to select the right stock for yourself, you want to be specialist and very much sure why are you selecting the stock, you should have very compressive understand of stock .Focus investing and selecting a good stock have enormous power and nobody does it , in value investment if you see Warren Buffett, even he is very focus in selecting right stock and specialist in four industries like banking, insurance, consumer non durable & media, his returns in those area very good.

By doing this you can easily outperformed the market by following value investing process. Look for a cheap and ugly will be a critical ingredient of a successful search strategy, the stocks that are obscure; here are also quite a few companies that haven't received the same attention. Many of these businesses have tremendous growth potential, and despite their relative obscurity, make great potential investments, for the time when financial market is falling apart or is the industry is in real trouble or the company is in real trouble and things will be revamp and again in the same place, this is where the real treasure and abundance of wealth for you to grab.

The cheap stock in the portfolio will always outperformed the market, look for cheap, ugly, otherwise ignored stock and stay away for glamour over valued stock. If you are portfolio manager and you see other are buying the glamour stock and if you don't buy , you may lose the client , and result will be your portfolio will perform low compare with cheap and ugly stock .For the marketing prospective they buy famous stock with high valuation , this is the first step to be a value investor.

When you sell stock, the other side is buying stock and you are selling because the stock will go down compare to other side is buying because the stock will perform, the other side is motivated because of the psychological, as the other side seller of the trade is always wrong.

We should learn from the 2000 tech boom, where all investor is acting as heading mentality, buying tech stock to gain high return, the big tech stocks was coved with analysts, predicting the earnings. You have to know what you know and what you don't know as we call circle of competence as Warren Buffett is very specific about his competence. All the stock is not measurable and we cannot take advantage of all the stock listed.

In the search of good stock idea, there are some biases that are as follows: -

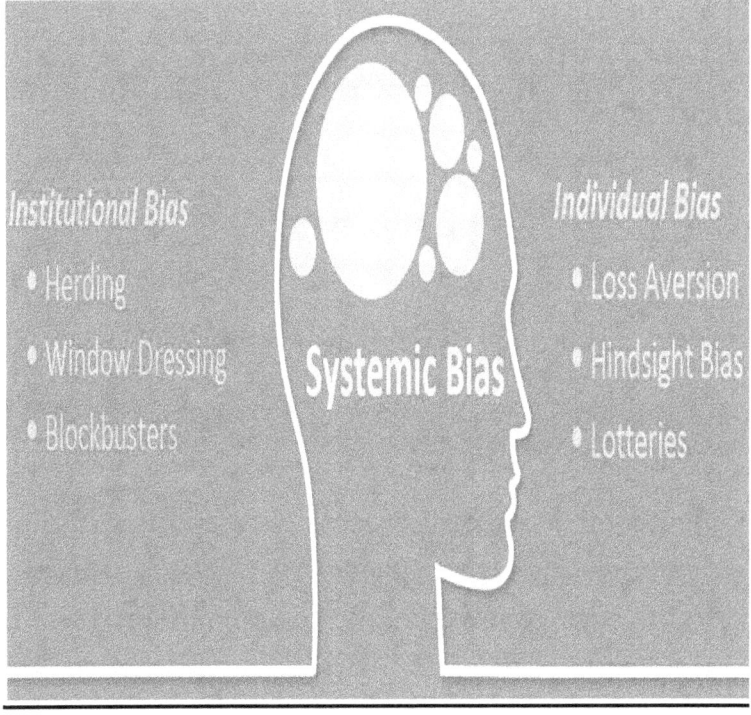

Systemic bias

Institutional Bias
- Herding
- Window Dressing
- Blockbusters

Individual Bias
- Loss Aversion
- Hindsight Bias
- Lotteries

We will go through the details of how this bias effect in selecting the good stock.

Systemic bias, also called institutional bias, is the inherent tendency of a process to support particular outcomes. The term generally refers to human systems such as institutions; the equivalent bias in non-human systems (such as measurement instruments or mathematical models used to estimate physical quantities) is often called systematic bias, and leads to systematic error in measurements or estimates. The issues of systemic bias are dealt with extensively in the field of industrial organization economics.

Institutional Bias

A tendency for the procedures and practices of particular institutions to operate in ways which result in certain social groups being advantaged or favoured and others being disadvantaged or devalued. This need not be the result of any conscious prejudice or discrimination but rather of the majority simply following existing rules or norms.

- **Herding**

    Herd bias, also known as the 'bandwagon effect', is a psychological phenomenon in which people rationalise that a course of action is the right one because 'everybody else' is doing it. In the world of investment, this can take the form of panic buying or selling.

- **Window Dressing**

    Window dressing is a strategy used by mutual fund and other portfolio managers near the year or quarter end to improve the appearance of a fund's performance before presenting it to clients or shareholders. To window dress, the fund manager sells stocks with large losses and purchases high-flying stocks near the end of the quarter. These securities are then reported as part of the fund's holdings.

- **Blockbusters**
Investor focus on the buying the hot stock that can be the next game changer a blockbuster stock like Apple or Amazon ,they make mistake at buying at right price and not making good return from the stock .

Individual Bias

Individual biases can be either cognitive, such as overconfidence, or motivational, such as wishful thinking. In addition, when making judgements in groups, decision makers and experts might be affected by group-level biases.

- **Loss Aversion**

    In cognitive psychology and decision theory, loss aversion refers to people's tendency to prefer avoiding losses to acquiring equivalent gains: it is better to not lose $5 than to find $5. The principle is very prominent in the domain of economics.

- **Hindsight Bias**

    Hindsight bias, also known as the knew-it-all-along phenomenon or creeping determinism, refers to the common tendency for people to perceive events that have already occurred as having been more predictable than they actually were before the events took place.

- **Lotteries**

    People buy lotteries to become quick rich same applicable with the rosy stock, same applicable to people buy stock, which is hot and investor love it. When it comes to lotteries, winners are often highly publicised. This can have a long-lasting impression. You might, for example, find yourself wondering "If they can do it, why can't I?" which makes the idea that wins are regular appealing, when in fact they are rare.

8
Valuation

"The Heart of Value Investing"

We are going to talk about the Graham & Dodd value investing process as we want to value the business effectively. When you go to Wall Street, what you will see that mostly of the analyst Value Company , they estimate of cash flow and ratio analysis ,these are the most common type of valuation, as lot of MBA students learn this in there course and use it to do the valuation of the company and yet fail to get the desired result .Analyst use lots of multiple matrix , cash flow , added back Amortization to EBIT , it is a relative valuation   , then they compare with the similar company trading in the exchange and DCF (Discounted Cash Flow)

"If you can look into the seeds of time, and say which grain will grow and which will not, speak then unto me."

--William Shakespeare

Charlie Munger said at the 1996 Berkshire Hathaway Annual Meeting: *"Warren talks about these discounted cash flows. I've never seen him do one."*

Warren Buffett: All investing is laying out cash now to get some more back in the future. The concept of "a bird in the hand" came from Aesop in about 600 BC. He knew a lot, but not that [he lived in] 600 BC. He couldn't know everything. [Laughter] The question is how many birds...

All the company have different relative valuation, as strong economic positions company should have higher multiples, you cannot judge the management only based on the valuation, if multiple is high, indicate management is performing super.

Drawback of Relative valuation

Relative valuation is a simple way to unearth low-priced companies with strong fundamentals. As such, investors use comparative multiples like the price-earnings ratio (P/E), enterprise multiple (EV/EBITDA) and price-to-book ratio (P/B) all the time to assess the relative worth and performance of companies, as well as identify buy and sell opportunities. The trouble is that while relative valuation is quick and easy to use, it can be a trap for investors.

Investors need to be cautious with stocks that are proclaimed to be "inexpensive." More often than not, the argument for buying a supposedly undervalued stock isn't that the company has a strong balance sheet, excellent products or a competitive advantage. Trouble is, the company might look undervalued because it's trading in an overvalued sector.

Tech Bubbles 2008 when a market is valuing an entire sector incorrectly, relative valuation can be inaccurate.

"Those who have knowledge don't predict. Those who predict don't have knowledge."
--Lao Tzu, *6th Century BC Chinese Poet*

Drawback of Discounted cash Flow

Discounted cash flow (DCF) is a valuation method used to estimate the value of an investment based on its future cash flows. DCF analysis attempts to figure out the value of an investment today, based on projections of how much money it will generate in the future.

$$DCF = \frac{CF_1}{(1+r)^1} + \frac{CF_2}{(1+r)^2} + \ldots + \frac{CF_n}{(1+r)^n}$$

Cash Flow (CF) Cash Flow is a method of estimating what an asset is worth today by using projected cash flows.

Discount Rate (r) for business valuation purposes, the discount rate is typically a firm's Weighted Average Cost of Capital (WACC). Investors use WACC because it represents the required rate of return that investors expect from investing in the company.

Period Number (n) ach cash flow is associated with a time period. Common time periods are years, quarters, or months.

Free cash flow is the cash a company produces through its operations, less the cost of expenditures on assets. In other words, free cash flow (FCF) is the cash left over after a company pays for its operating expenses and capital expenditures, also known as CAPEX

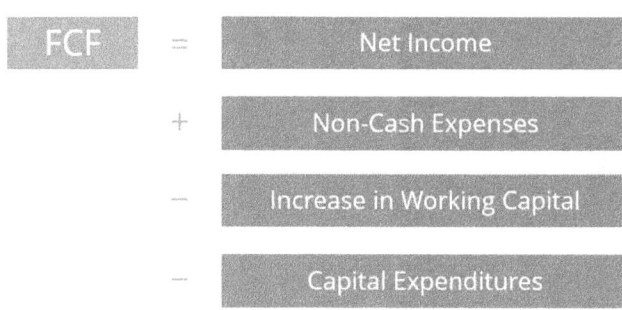

- Valuation obtained is very sensitive to a large number of assumptions/forecasts, and can thus vary over a wide range

- Often very time-intensive relative to some other valuation techniques.

- Involves forecasting future performance, which is very difficult.

- Operating Cash Flow Projections The first and most important factor in calculating the DCF value of a stock is estimating the series of operating cash flow projections. There are a number of inherent problems with earnings and cash flow forecasting that can generate problems with DCF analysis. The most prevalent is that the uncertainty with cash flow projection increases for each year in the forecast— and DCF models often use five or even 10 years' worth of estimates. The outer years of the model can be total shots in the dark.

- Capital Expenditure Projections Free cash flow projection involves projecting capital expenditures for each model year. Again, the degree of uncertainty increases with each additional year in the model.

- Discount Rate and Growth Rate Perhaps the most contentious assumptions in a DCF model are the discount rate and growth rate assumptions. There are many ways to approach the discount rate in an equity DCF model. Analysts might use the Markowitzian $R = Rf + \beta(Rm - Rf)$ or maybe the weighted average cost of capital of the firm as the discount rate in the DCF model. Both approaches are quite theoretical and may not work well in real-world investing applications. Other investors may choose to use an arbitrary standard hurdle rate to evaluate all equity investments

- DCF analysis has increased in popularity as more analysts focus on corporate cash flow as a key determinant in whether a company is able to do things to enhance share value. it is one of the few equity valuation tools that can provide a real, intrinsic value against which to compare current stock price as opposed to a relative value comparing one stock to other stocks in the same sector or to the market's overall performance. Market analysts observe that it is hard to fake cash flow.

People just carelessly use multiple in valuations, they say this company is 10 X if EBITDA OR 20 X multiple and if you are doing that you should be very clear that everybody is also doing that and there is no advantage either .What B-school teach in DCF is to estimate the revenue year by year and the margin year by year and make assumption about business performance , there investment , there sustainability , management competence , they estimate the cost of capital WACC and discount to the Net present value .whole life people do Discounted cash flow and forecasting for 15 , 10 or 15 years .when you do DCF who will find all the value is the terminal value , and the terminal value which stand in for future cash flow for five or seven years, is the estimated year of cash flow .The standard growth rate is 10 % and WACC is 5 % , if there is changes in growth rate or WACC ,for a value investor this estimate is a joke .In DCF there is no contribution of the balance sheet .

Balance sheet is the heart of a company, a strong balance sheet is treasure for the investor and valuating a balance sheet is acute rather than estimating cash flow. if you don't know the balance sheet of the company then it is not a good to value a company. In DCF you are talking very good information of the near-term cash flow and very bad information is DCF and add it together, and when we add bad information to good information, we get the bad result.

Take example of assumption we make in estimating General Motors while doing DCF for 10 years, what all we should know: -

- *What are the profit margins?*
- *What are the sales?*
- *What will be the sales growth rate?*
- *What will be the level of investment?*
- *What will be cost of capital?*

How many people, investor or analysts know that all this for next 10 or 15 years compare of if we value the balance sheet of the General Motors which will be prefect to examine the valuation.

In using DCF it is very difficult to say that the cash flow is sustainable? The entire research analyst all DCF valuation whole day and prediction the future which is unknown and that the reason Warren Buffett have $88 billion net worth .DCF is theoretically right to do but no particle. (Charlie Munger used the metaphor: *"When you mix turds with raisins, you get turds."*)

While doing valuation we need to keep in mind and ask our self: -

- That the industry we are doing is economically viable, Economic viability of an industry refers to the situation when demand and supply curves of the industry meet at some positive level of output. But if demand curve and supply curve do not intersect each other at any positive quantity, the industry is economically non-viable. In such a situation, supply curve lies above the demand curve.

- Competitive advantage – the company sell a unique product or unique service like Coca Cola, Hershey.

- Sustainable competitive advantage – company should have product will be there after 10 years or 20 years with increase in sales and owing a piece of the consumer's mind.

- Growth in industry with moats – business growth with no low competition and barriers to entry for growth.

You should have confidence on your valuation; the valuation is not on predicting assumption but on strategic assumption.

The valuation process shared by the, Benjamin Graham Security Analysis with David Dodd, was published in 1934 till today it is the most relevant valuation that has created enormous wealth .

The Valuation has Three Elements to Value a business.

1. Asset value (AV)

2. Earnings power value (EPV)

3. Franchise value (FV)

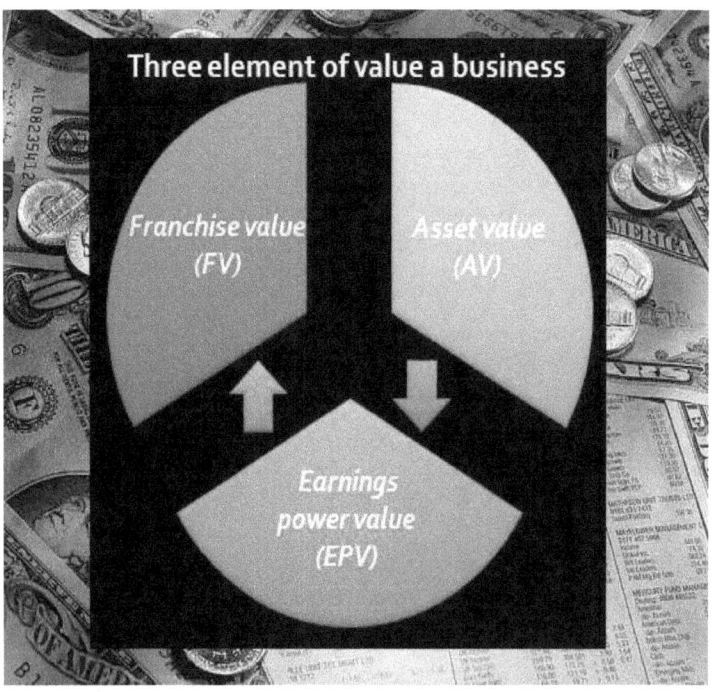

Asset Value (AV)

We will start the valuation with assets; reason is that assets are tangible. We can go to the details of balance sheet .Start with assets value and this is most reliable information we have about the company in whichever industry company operates in, we can do the valuation in two ways one is the liquidation, the company which is going to be liquidate , we need to do dept valuation of each assets its liquidate value , which assets is recoverable in other hand the second valuation we can do is the will be there and have the viability and will perform ,then we need to know , how to value such company .

Once we will value the assets then we will go forward to value the current earning, we will see in two parts, first if there is growth and when there is no growth in earning, the current earning can be forecast able, can the earning be sustainable and will remain good in the future.

A balance sheet is a statement of the financial position of a business that lists the assets, liabilities, and owner's equity at a particular point in time. In other words, the balance sheet illustrates your business's net worth.

The balance sheet may also have details from previous years so you can do a back-to-back comparison of two consecutive years. This data will help you track your performance and will identify ways to build up your finances and see where you need to improve. You can also use the balance sheet to determine how to meet your financial obligations and figure out the best ways to use credit to finance your operations.

The balance sheet is the most important of the three main financial statements used to illustrate the financial health of a business.

A Simple Balance Sheet

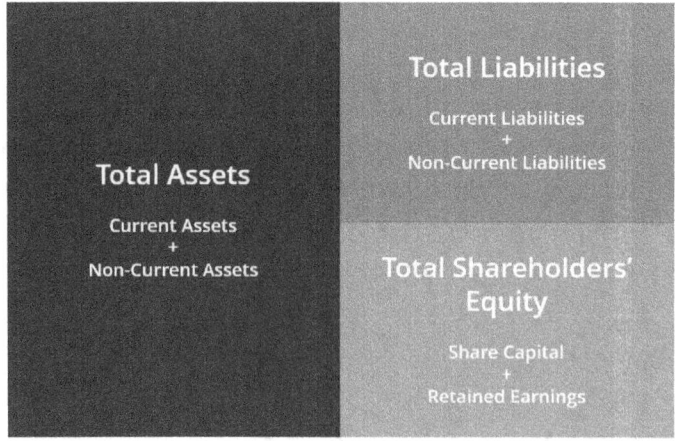

We will value the assets in two parts

1. Tangible Assets
2. Intangible Assets

Tangible Assets

There are two types of categories of assets called tangible and intangible assets. Tangible assets are typically physical assets or property owned by a company, such as computer equipment. Tangible assets are the main type of assets that companies use to produce their product and service.

Intangible Assets

Intangible assets don't physically exist, yet are they have a monetary value since they represent potential revenue. A type of an intangible asset could be a copyright to a song. The record company that owns the copyright would get paid a royalty each time the song is played. Intangible assets things such as intellectual property, trademarks, patents.

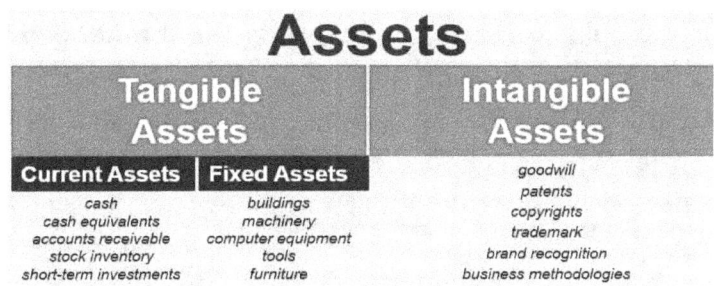

We will check in our valuation that what the earning company are is generating from the assets, are management capable to utilise the assets correctly, we see how company leadership position in the industry in their assets deployment.

In assets valuation we will see how much current value of the assets that you will be willing to pay for the tangible and intangible assets and some of the assets will be not be reflecting in the balance sheet, those value are the brand value, 'Brand equity' is a phrase used in the marketing industry refers to the perceived worth of a brand in and of itself—i.e., the social value of a well-known brand name. It is based on the idea that the owner of a well-known brand name can generate more revenue simply from brand recognition, as consumers perceive the products of well-known brands as better than those of lesser-known brands. In other words, brand equity refers to the branding of a product name on an attention-deficit public, Brand value, on the other hand, is the financial worth of the brand. To determine brand value, businesses need to estimate how much the brand is worth in the market – in other words, how much would someone purchasing the brand pay? Warren Buffett like brand companies such as Coca Cola, Bank of American and Apple Inc. Brands are very essential for the increase and profit for an operating business.

Earnings Power value (EPV)

Once we will do with the Assets value (AV), we will move further to Earning Power Value, what kind of Profit Company is generating from those sales? What kind of expenses company is generating? The kind of deprecation charging yearly basic? What will be the sustainable earning after adjusting the deprecation?

Franchise value (FV)

This is our third step to value a company, how much we are ready to pay for the growth of the company, after understanding the strategic analyses of the company.

The Three Elements

As we have understood assets value has two branches tangible and intangible assets as we understand balance sheet, we can able to value the assets reproduction value.

We need to go through all the financial report of the company, mainly balance sheet to know what company real market current value.

Going forward we will read the income statement to find out where earning is generating, those earning are sustainable and can we forecast the earning. In this way we will do the valuation of the company.

We will see AV compare with the EPV and decide shall we should invest in the company or wait for the right time. We will check current market value of the company with our estimated AV and EPV and analyse do we have enough margin of safety to buy with discounted value and investment will be risk free.

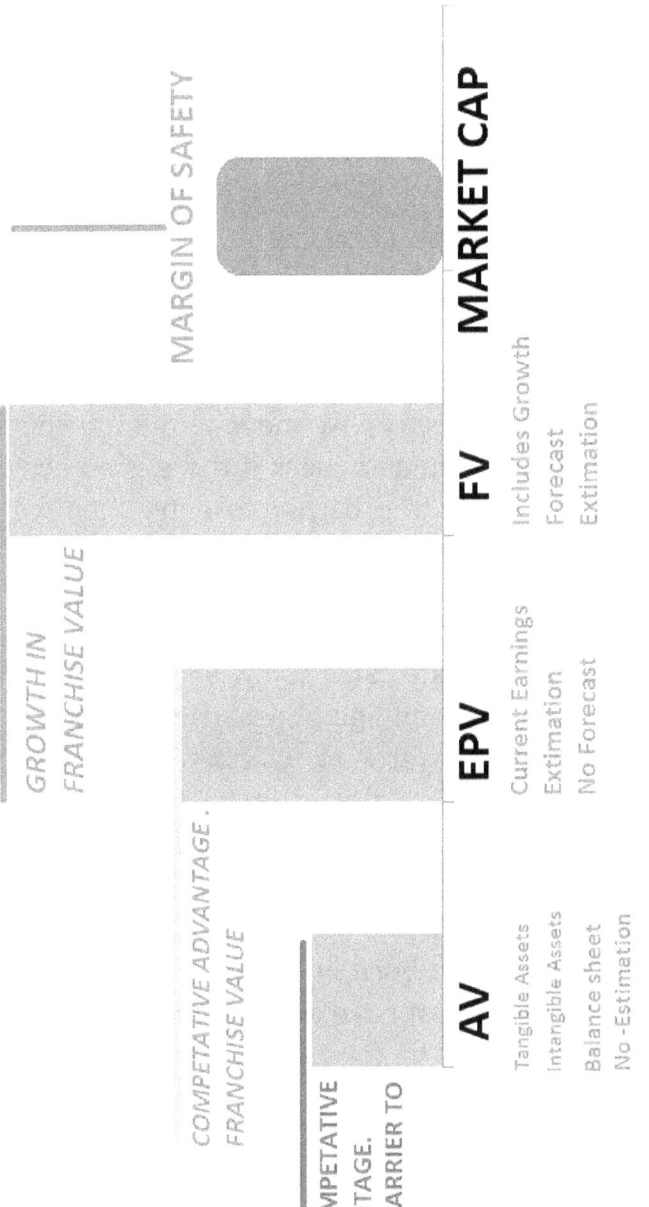

9

Barriers to Entry

If the Earning Power value is not above the Asset value, then, there is no growth in the earning as company is not utilising the assets properly. We have to ask our self before we move to the franchise Value, we need to stop and check if there is no competitive advantage and free barrier to entry then we should not calculate the Franchise Value because company is not creating any value to the shareholders.

If company create value to the shareholders and have competitive advantage and barrier to entry then we can move forward to calculate Franchise Value. Modern value investor estimate that company enjoy barrier to entry and they check franchise value, are company is having above return on equity and return on capital employed, do company have free cash flow and no need to borrow money and pay high cost of capital, they must have enough cash to fund them self for the growth of the company and create value to their shareholders.

ASSETS VALUE

EARNING POWER VALUE

AV >EPV NO BARRIERS TO ENTRY
AV<EPV BARRIERS TO ENTRY

MOVE TO
FRANCHISE VALUE

NO FRANCHISE VALUE STOP

Compare Assets Value with Earning Power Value.

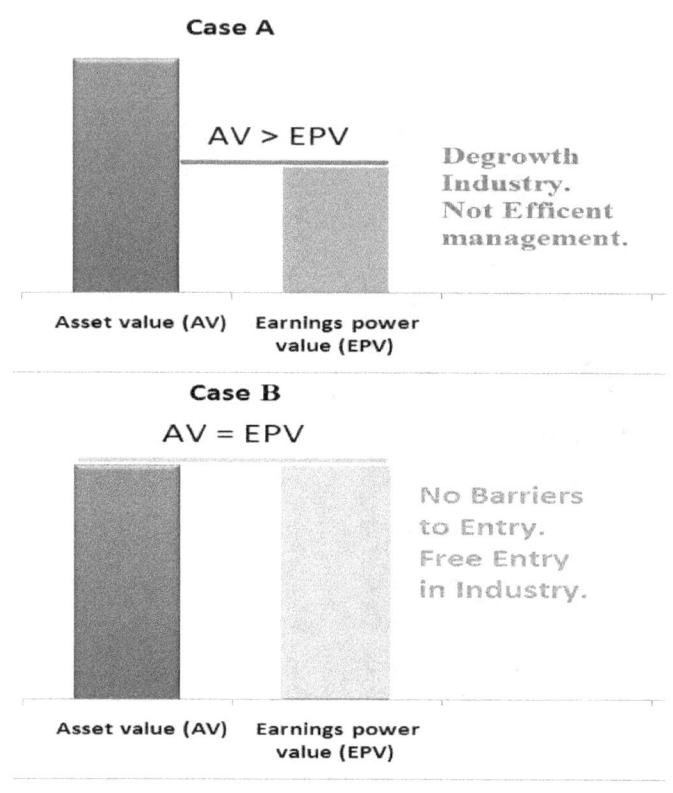

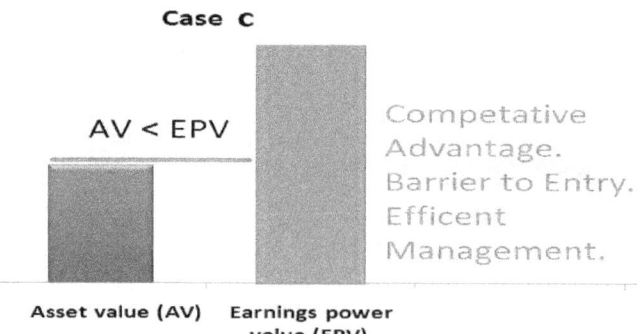

We value the company in different ways and see that able to understand what and how company is using its assets to generate earning, Let understand one by one all three cases.

AV is Greater Than EPV

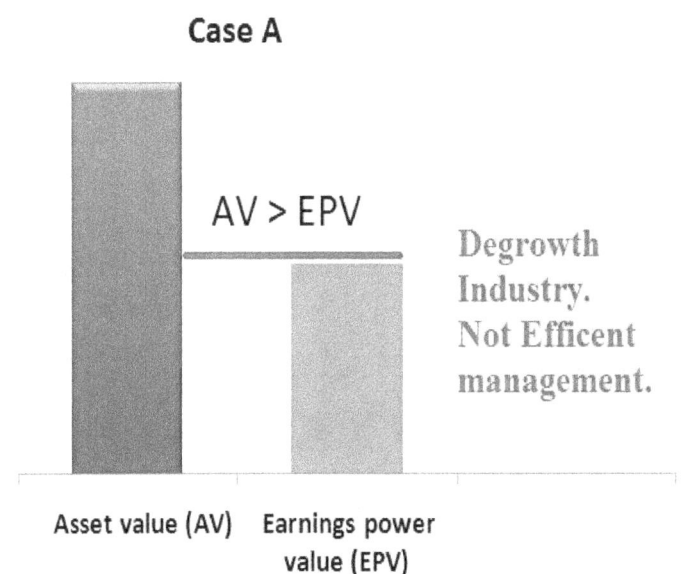

If you see the assets is greater than the Earning power value it indicate that the industry in which company is operating is in decline mode like automobiles industry, or newspapers, you don't find the growth in the company and need intensive huge capital to operate, the second thought we can have is the competence of management, the management cannot able to utilise the assets in an effective manner to generate earning about the cost of assets .We can always say there is an issue with the management , in this situation , the company might not able to sustain in long run , this valuation is best above all the valuation we have learn , you won't find this in DCF valuation .

AV Equals EPV

Case B
AV = EPV

No Barriers to Entry. Free Entry in Industry.

Asset value (AV)   Earnings power value (EPV)

In this situation the assets value is equal to the earning power value it indicate that the company is generating equal earning compare with its assets, as such there is no barrier to entry, any new company can enter the industry, some industry there is no competitive advantages such as automobiles, real state, commodity type product like airline.

There is free market, company can replace other company, management is just making enough earning as per the assets value they have, not able to utilise the value of assets.

EPV in Excess to AV

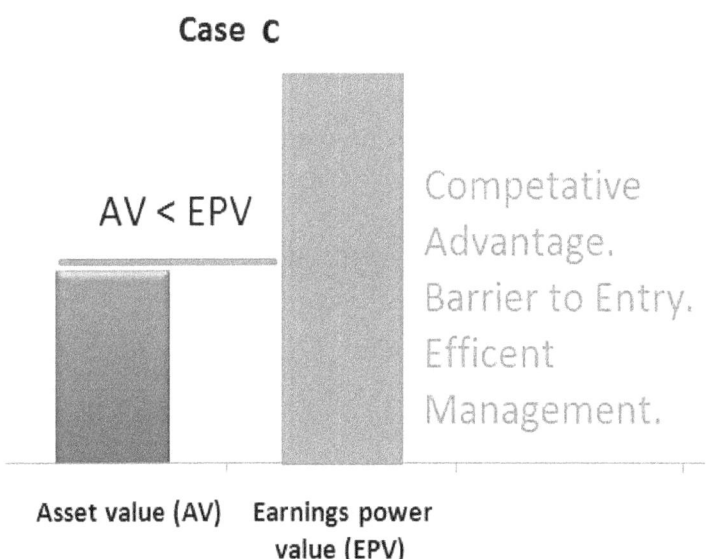

In the Case C we see Earning Power Value is Greater than the Assets value, it indicate that company enjoy the competitive advantage and there is a barrier to entry, or in other terms we can say moats, which value investor Warren Buffett like to invest, it indicate that company have the superior management and create value to the shareholders by utilising the assets properly to generate the earning above the assets value such company like Apple, Microsoft & Visa.

Qualitative and Quantitative Analysis

Our investment approach in value investing we will go through the both Qualitative and Quantitative Analysis.

Qualitative Analysis fundamentally means to measure something by its quality rather than quantity. When we do qualitative analysis, we are exploring how we describe something. Very often, we cannot use numbers or numerical expressions to describe those things. When we do qualitative work, we work with descriptions. We work with feelings, thoughts, and perceptions. We attempt to understand motivations and behaviours and positive associations with a brand, management trustworthiness, customer satisfaction, competitive advantage, we will go through how competitor perform in the industry, how company is operating in the industry, the position of the company in the industry.

Quantitative Analysis is the opposite; to measure by quantity rather than quality. When we do quantitative analysis, we are exploring facts, measures, numbers and percentages. When we do quantitative work, we work with numbers, statistics, formula and data. We will go deep in income statement and balance sheet and will give you measurements to confirm each problem or opportunity and understand it. We will see ratio analyses and some matrix like ROE.

10

The Framework of Value Investing

1. Asset value (AV)
2. Earnings power value (EPV)
3. Franchise value (FV)

Asset value (AV)

In the Balance Sheet we have Assets = Liability + Equity, in the assets side we have property plant and equipment cash, inventories, investment etc and in the Liability side we have account payable, debts, other liabilities and equity.

We will do deep understanding of balance sheet assets side, the value which hidden like Brands etc we will include all those while doing the valuation.

Balance sheet

Assets

Tangible Assets
- Cash
- Property Plant & Equipment's
- Inventories
- Receivable Etc

Intangible Assets
- Brands
- Patients
- Trademark

Liabilities

- Debts short Term and Long Term
- Equity
- Off Balance sheet
- Lawsuits etc

How much we are willing to pay for these assets? When company buy the assets, it could be tangible and intangible assets, that they have paid the price, the time it was purchased like plant, land, building, acquire another brand.

All you need to do is to revalue the all assets the company owns and value it to the current market price.

We should value first the assets company own, we need to do over all analysis qualitative to understand that is the company is in distress than best approach would be liquidation approach, how much we can get from the distressed assets, but in case company have a sustainable approach, we will do the valuation on a reproduction basis, how much is the value of the reproduction assets.

When we will finish the value of different assets, than we will move further to book value of the equity and add all the assets adjustment we have made, we will add current assets, PPE, goodwill and then will add all the missing intangible like product portfolio company have different product to sell, value of the customer, there number of workforces, there is a cost to empower employee and any other, than we will adjust those value to get total assets value.

Book value of Assets

+ Adjustment
- Current Assets value
- Property Plant and Equipment
- Goodwill

+Intangibles
- Product Portfolio
- Customers
- Workforce

+ Subsidiaries

= Total Assets Value

Value of Assets

- Cash
- Marketable Securities
- Accounts Receivable
- Inventories

Total Current Assets

- Property, Plant ,and Equipment's ,Net
- Goodwill
- Deferred Tax
- Investment in affiliate

Missing Intangibles
- Product Portfolio
- Brand –Customers
- Workforces
- Other intangibles

Total Assets

Current Assets

Current assets have a lifespan of one year or less, meaning they can be converted easily into cash. Such asset classes include cash and cash equivalents, accounts receivable and inventory. Cash, the most fundamental of current assets, also includes non-restricted bank accounts and checks. Cash equivalents are very safe assets that can be readily converted into cash; U.S. Treasuries are one such example. Account's receivables consist of the short-term obligations owed to the company by its clients. Companies often sell products or services to customers on credit; these obligations are held in the current assets account until they are paid off by the clients.

Lastly, inventory represents the company's raw materials, work-in-progress goods and finished goods. Depending on the company, the exact makeup of the inventory account will differ. For example, a manufacturing firm will carry a large number of raw materials, while a retail firm carries none. The makeup of a retailer's inventory typically consists of goods purchased from manufacturers and wholesalers.

Non-Current Assets

Non-current assets are assets that are not turned into cash easily, are expected to be turned into cash within a year, and/or have a lifespan of more than a year. They can refer to tangible assets, such as machinery, computers, buildings and land. Non-current assets also can be intangible assets, such as goodwill, patents or copyright. While these assets are not physical in nature, they are often the resources that can make or break a company – the value of a brand name, for instance, should not be underestimated.

Adjustment

Cash --

Cash and cash equivalents under the current assets section of a balance sheet represent the amount of money the company has in the bank, whether in the form of cash, savings bonds, certificates of deposit, or money invested in money market funds. It tells you how much money is available to the business immediately.

The cash having required minimal adjustment in valuation, as we believe that the company stating right information to the investor as it is been audited.

Marketable Securities --

Marketable securities are liquid financial instruments that can be quickly converted into cash at a reasonable price. The liquidity of marketable securities comes from the fact that the maturities tend to be less than one year, and that the rates at which they can be bought or sold have little effect on prices. These short-term liquid securities can be bought or sold on a public stock exchange or a public bond exchange.

These securities tend to mature in a year or less and can be either debt or equity. Marketable securities include common stock, Treasury bills, and money market instruments, among others.

We will treat same valuation as we used in valuating cash, as we have right information from the company about the securities, in case we found the information shared by the company is not true, we may get back to the company and do investigation.

Accounts Receivable –

Accounts receivable are legally enforceable claims for payment held by a business for goods supplied and/or services rendered that customers/client have ordered but not paid for. These are generally in the form of invoices raised by a business and delivered to the customer for payment within an agreed time frame.

Account's receivable is shown in a balance sheet as an asset. It is one of a series of accounting transactions dealing with the billing of a customer for goods and services that the customer has ordered. These may be distinguished from notes receivable, which are debts created through formal legal instruments called promissory notes.

Accounts receivable is the balance of money due to a firm for goods or services delivered or used but not yet paid for by customers. Account's receivables are listed on the balance sheet as a current asset. AR is any amount of money owed by customers for purchases made on credit. In valuation it will be treat as same value.

Inventories—

Inventory or stock is the goods and materials that a business holds for the ultimate goal of resale. Inventory management is a discipline primarily about specifying the shape and placement of stocked goods; it will treat as a default.

Property, Plant, and Equipment's, Net –

Net PP&E is short for Net Property Plant and Equipment. Property Plant and Equipment is the value of all buildings, land, furniture, and other physical capital that a business has purchased to run its business. The term "Net" means that it is "Net" of accumulated depreciation expenses.

Property, plant, and equipment (PP&E) are long-term assets vital to business operations and not easily converted into cash. Property, plant, and equipment are tangible assets, meaning they are physical in nature or can be touched. The total value of PP&E can range from very low to extremely high compared to total assets.

We have to revalue the Property, plant, and equipment to the current market value because if the company have bought the land and building log back around 30 years ago, the price of the assets has been increased and that is not reflecting in the balance sheet, balance sheet takes the value, when it was purchased.

While calculation the reproduction value of PPE that include

- *Land*
- *Building*
- *Plant & Machinery*
- *Fixture*
- *Vehicle*
- *Office Equipment's*
- *Other – In Progress.*

Now we need to know how to value

- **Land**

    Land value is the value of a piece of property including both the value of the land itself as well as any improvements that have been made to it. This is not to be confused with site value, which is the reasonable value of the land assuming that there are no leases, mortgages or anything else present that would otherwise change the site's value. Land values increase when demand for land exceeds the supply of available land or if a particular piece of land has intrinsic value greater than neighbouring areas. We will take 25 % above the land value and if in case we know the value of Land in current market, we will take that value.

- **Building**

  The cost of the building will be appreciating as the cost of the construction is increasing every year so while valuing the company take 25% above the value of building.

- **Plant & Machinery**

  The plant and machinery are a deprecating asset, the value will remain reducing as the machine have a certain life, after that it become unusable or scrap, in this we need to value the machine and we don't know that, how long company is using the machinery and plant.

  First Method to value, an ideal machine life is eight to ten years so we will take 10 years, we assume there is 9 % deprecating in the value of the machinery, so to calculate that value below the working.

  Suppose the Plant and Machinery value is $7700 and we deprecate for ten years for 9 %, we will get the reproduction value to $2999.

Year	Depricate	$ 7,700
1	9%	$ 7,007
2	9%	$ 6,376
3	9%	$ 5,802
4	9%	$ 5,280
5	9%	$ 4,805
6	9%	$ 4,373
7	9%	$ 3,979
8	9%	$ 3,621
9	9%	$ 3,295
10	9%	$ 2,999

Second Method to value Plant and Machine is just to deprecate with 60 %, you will get value close to $3080.

- Fixture, Vehicle and Office Equipment's need to deprecate Furniture, fixtures, and equipment (abbreviated FF&E or FFE) are movable furniture, fixtures, or other equipment that have no permanent connection to the structure of a building or utilities. These items depreciate substantially over their long-term use, but they are important costs to consider when valuing a company, especially during liquidation procedures.

  Examples of FF&E include desks, chairs, computers, electronic equipment, tables, bookcases, and partitions. Sometimes the term furniture, fixtures, and accessories (FF&A) is used in place of FF&E. We will deprecate it to **50 %** of the value to get the reproduction cost.

- **Other – In Progress.**

    Some work is ongoing within the company so we will consider same value for the reproduction cost.

Goodwill –

Goodwill is an intangible asset that is associated with the purchase of one company by another. Specifically, goodwill is the portion of the purchase price that is higher than the sum of the net fair value of all of the assets purchased in the acquisition and the liabilities assumed in the process. The value of a company's brand name, solid customer base, good customer relations, good employee relations, and proprietary technology

- Goodwill is an intangible asset that accounts for the excess purchase price of another company.
- Items included in goodwill are proprietary or intellectual property and brand recognition, which are not easily quantifiable.

- Goodwill is calculated by taking the purchase price of a company and subtracting the difference between the fair market value of the assets and liabilities.
- Companies are required to identify the value of goodwill on their financial statements at least once a year and record any impairment.

We will value the goodwill zero; we will minus the goodwill in assets valuation.

Deferred Tax—

A deferred tax liability occurs when a business has a certain amount of income for an accounting period and that amount is different from the taxable amount on their tax return. When the amount is less than the estimated tax, an entry is placed on the balance sheet in the form of a liability. No adjustment in valuation.

Investment in affiliate--

For corporate, securities and capital markets, an affiliate is a person or entity directly or indirectly controlling, being controlled by, or under common control with another person or entity. In many cases of foreign direct investment (FDI), companies create subsidiaries and affiliates in host countries, no adjustment require.

Missing Intangibles

Product Portfolio—

A product portfolio is the collection of all the products or services offered by a company to their customer to generate revenue. A company may develop their unique and have known the process and we need to value their product; the amount company have invested to developed their product.

Need to calculate the R&D expenses multiply by number of products to get the value, the company is making, we need to see how much they are doing expenses in the R&D and multiple with the product portfolio to get the product valuation.

Brand –Customers --

Brand loyalty is the positive association consumers attach to a particular product or brand. Customers that exhibit brand loyalty are devoted to a product or service, which is demonstrated by their repeat purchases despite competitor's efforts to lure them away. Corporations invest significant amounts of money on customer service and marketing to create and maintain brand loyalty for an established product. Coca-Cola Company is an example of an iconic brand that has resulted in customers demonstrating brand loyalty over the years despite Pepsi's products and marketing efforts.

Company makes huge investment in creating the brands, strong brand is a heart of the company. we will value in worth of the brand, brands like apple it's almost hard to get a sense of the scale of a company like Apple It is the most profitable company on earth. It was the first company with a trillion-dollar market cap, and remains one of the most valuable companies by that measure. And for the ninth year in a row, it's also the most valuable brand in the world ever.

At least that's according to Forbes, which recently released its rankings of the most valuable brands. That report has the value of Apple's brand as $205 billion. The brand not the company.

That means the value of the tangible and intangible assets associated with what makes Apple, is the highest of any company ever. There are some other great brands on the list too. Google is on there. Microsoft and Amazon are near the top. Even Facebook rounds out the top five.

But none of them are anywhere near the value of Apple's brand, which is the first to top $200 billion.
To approach to value a brand is to check how much a company have expenses in marketing for their brands then we will capitalise those expenses with the cost of the capital.

- If the company in the manufacturing industry and don't have the brand value then we will calculate the sales commission what company is paying to its dealer multiple with the revenue

- If company have brand s like apple or Microsoft the valuation will be the marketing expenses or advertisement expenses divided by the cost of capital to get the value.

Workforces—

The workforce or labour force is the labour pool in employment. It is generally used to describe those working for a single company or industry, but can also apply to a geographic region like a city, state, or country. Within a company, its value can be labelled as its "Workforce in Place"

We need to know how much a company need to pay to reproduce the workforce, work force divides in two category blue collar and white collar. White collar workers are not easy to replace as they have more skills like doctor, scientist white collar reproduce cost around 20%, blue collar manpower to be value around 10-15%.

There is a cost to reproduce the manpower.

11

Valuation of Apple Inc

Founded   April 1, 1976; 44 years ago

Apple Inc. is an American multinational technology company headquartered in Cupertino, California, that designs, develops, and sells consumer electronics, computer software, and online services. It is considered one of the Big Four technology companies, alongside Amazon, Google, and Microsoft.

Products:
The Company designs, manufactures and markets mobile communication and media devices, personal computers and portable digital music players, and sells a variety of related software, services, accessories, networking solutions and third-party digital content and applications. The Company's products and services include iPhone®, iPad®, Mac®,

iPod®, Apple Watch®, Apple TV®, a portfolio of consumer and professional software applications, iOS, macOS™, watchOS® and tvOS™ operating systems, iCloud®, Apple Pay® and a variety of accessory, service and support offerings. The Company sells and delivers digital content and applications through the iTunes Store®, App Store®, Mac App Store, TV App Store, iBooks Store™ and Apple Music® (collectively "Internet Services").

Customers:

The Company's customers are primarily in the consumer, small and mid-sized business, and education, enterprise and government markets. The Company sells its products and resells third-party products in most of its major markets directly to consumers and small and mid-sized businesses through its retail and online stores and its direct sales force. The Company also employs a variety of indirect distribution channels, such as third-party cellular network carriers, wholesalers, retailers and value-added resellers. During 2016, the Company's net sales through its direct and indirect distribution channels accounted for 25% and 75%, respectively, of total net sales.

Apple's retail footprint has since expanded to 506 stores spanning 24 countries, including 272 in the U.S. and 234 combined in Australia, Austria, Belgium, Brazil, Canada, China, France, Hong Kong,

Apple Inc Balance Sheet

Apple Inc.

CONSOLIDATED BALANCE SHEETS
(In millions, except number of shares which are reflected in thousands and par value)

	September 29, 2018	September 30, 2017
ASSETS:		
Current assets:		
Cash and cash equivalents	$ 25,913	$ 20,289
Marketable securities	40,388	53,892
Accounts receivable, net	23,186	17,874
Inventories	3,956	4,855
Vendor non-trade receivables	25,809	17,799
Other current assets	12,087	13,936
Total current assets	131,339	128,645
Non-current assets:		
Marketable securities	170,799	194,714
Property, plant and equipment, net	41,304	33,783
Other non-current assets	22,283	18,177
Total non-current assets	234,386	246,674
Total assets	$ 365,725	$ 375,319
LIABILITIES AND SHAREHOLDERS' EQUITY:		
Current liabilities:		
Accounts payable	$ 55,888	$ 44,242
Other current liabilities	32,687	30,551
Deferred revenue	7,543	7,548
Commercial paper	11,964	11,977
Term debt	8,784	6,496
Total current liabilities	116,866	100,814
Non-current liabilities:		
Deferred revenue	2,797	2,836
Term debt	93,735	97,207
Other non-current liabilities	45,180	40,415
Total non-current liabilities	141,712	140,458
Total liabilities	258,578	241,272
Commitments and contingencies		
Shareholders' equity:		
Common stock and additional paid-in capital, $0.00001 par value: 12,600,000 shares authorized; 4,754,986 and 5,126,201 shares issued and outstanding, respectively	40,201	35,867
Retained earnings	70,400	98,330
Accumulated other comprehensive income/(loss)	(3,454)	(150)
Total shareholders' equity	107,147	134,047
Total liabilities and shareholders' equity	$ 365,725	$ 375,319

Assets Value (AV)

Let's look at the balance sheet, Apple Inc having $ 365.8 billion of assets and company are having $ 25.91 billion of Cash and cash equivalents, Property, plant, and equipment on a net basis is $41.3 billion, let look the assets as we have not found any goodwill in the balance sheet.

We need to check the missing intangible once we will complete the assets side, the book value of equity is $107.147 billion, and we will add book value of equity with the adjustment we made to know the assets value. We check income statement apple generate net income of $ 59.531 billion and seem a sustainable company, it's clearly state that apple have a future and it is not going to liquidate, so we will do the reproduction value of the assets.

Adjustment in Property, Plant, & Equipment's

Net Book Property, Plant, and Equipment's =$41.3 billion.

$Billion	2018
Land and buildings	16.2
Machinery, equipment and internal-use software	66.0
Leasehold improvements	8.2
Gross property, plant and equipment	90.4

Gross PPE

The First Adjustment

Property, Plant and Equipment, Net

$Billion		
Gross PPE	2018	Adjustment
Land and buildings	16.2	20.3
Machinery, equipment and internal-use software	66.0	26
Leasehold improvements	8.2	8.2
Gross property, plant and equipment	90.4	54.8

- Land and building as we are not having any information in the footnote on 10k report, we take the value same, some information is which all country they have invested in PPE in values.

	2018
Long-lived assets:	
U.S.	$ 23,963
China (1)	13,268
Other countries	4,073
Total long-lived assets	$ 41,304

We don't have much info about the Machinery, equipment and internal-use software so we have value it for 9 % and for 9 years.

Year	Depricate	$	66
1	9%	$	60
2	9%	$	55
3	9%	$	50
4	9%	$	45
5	9%	$	41
6	9%	$	37
7	9%	$	34
8	9%	$	31
9	9%	$	28
10	9%	$	26

Formula

Gross PPE = $54.8 - $41.3 = $13.5 billion.

It means we have additional $13.55 billion.

Adjustment in PPE = $13.55 Billion.

Adjustment in Goodwill

As we see in the assets side of the apple Inc, there is no goodwill it indicates that apple have not paid any value beyond of assets of any company to acquire. We will take the value of the goodwill zero and we don't know much about goodwill in balance sheet, in case company have any goodwill value in assets side, make sure you minus the value in the calculation of assets value.

Valuation of Missing Intangibles

Workforce –

We will see how many employees apple have and which state and what the average salary is for employee and we need to calculate the cost of reproducing the workforce.

Employees
As of September 29, 2018, the Company had approximately 132,000 full-time equivalent employees.

The Apple Selling, general and administrative is $16.7 Billion in which wages is included and in annual report we didn't find so we will search from other sources and decide the wages.

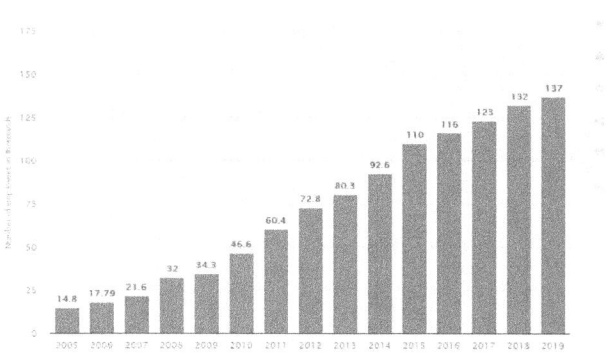
Apple's number of employees in the fiscal years 2005 to 2019 (in 1,000s)

Total work force = 137000

Calculation of the Workforce of Apple Inc

Total workforce: 137000
Average Wages : $30000
Total wages   : $4.11 Bilion
Take 20 % of $4.11 Billion

Workforce Value : $ 822 Million

Brand

There are ways to value the brand such as:

- You can discount the marketing expenses with the cost of capital of the company.
- You can search any recent any agency has done valuation of the brand, so we can have idea.

Apple Inc has not shared the annual Advertising Costs.

Advertising Costs

"Advertising costs are expensed as incurred and included in selling, general and administrative expenses."

The general and administrative is $16.7 Billion which include advertisement cost, Apple Inc don't share the advertising cost, as we are talking the cost of advertising from different sources, last 2016 the cost of advertising was $1.8 billion and after 4 years it must have increased as you can see in the graph, the cost is increasing yearly, so we take smooth value as we are taking $4 Billion of advertising Cost.

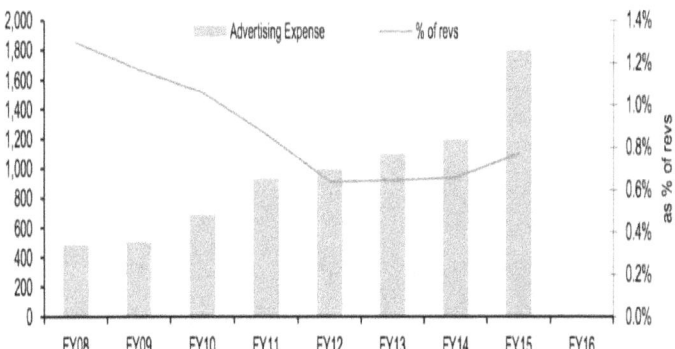

The cost of capital of Apple Inc

Competitive Comparison Data

Company	Market Cap (M)	WACC %
Apple Inc	$ 1,229,422.38	6.95
Samsung Electronics Co Ltd	$ 268,600.10	8.12
China Electronics Holding...	$ 124,978.90	0.00
Sony Corp	$ 76,040.18	5.08
Midea Group Co Ltd	$ 48,988.52	6.22
Gree Electric Appliances I...	$ 46,696.57	8.56
Xiaomi Corp	$ 32,027.30	0.00
Kyocera Corp	$ 20,065.15	7.42
Panasonic Corp	$ 16,729.95	4.75
Haier Smart Home Co Ltd	$ 13,680.73	7.64

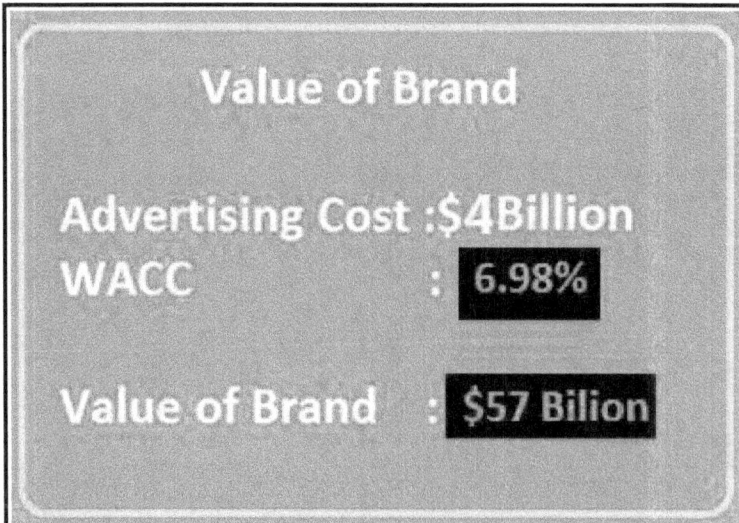

Value of Brand

Advertising Cost : $4Billion
WACC : 6.98%

Value of Brand : $57 Bilion

If we take other approach to value a brand we may seek for other reliable information.

We will take a smooth number of $80 Billion

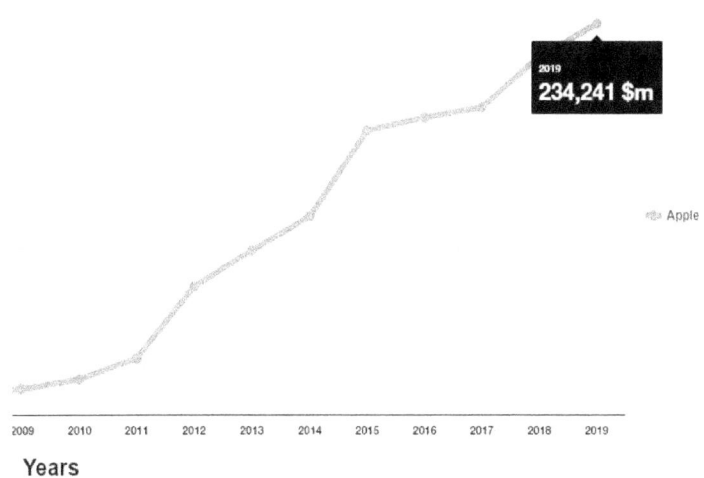

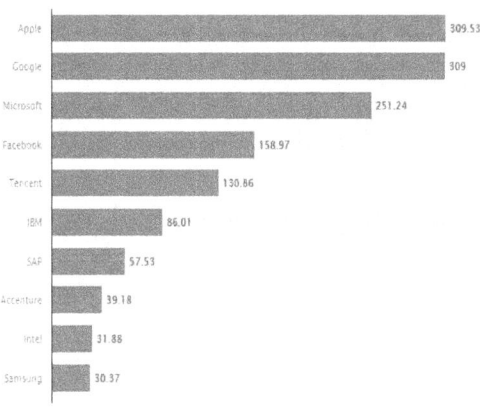

Values of the top 20 technology brands worldwide in 2019
(in billion U.S. dollars)

We have checked our valuation by the other companies listed the brand value of Apple Inc

- Forbes List -$206 Billion
- Statista   -$310 Billion
- Interbrand - $234 Billion

Product Line –

R&D expenses reported in 2018 were $14 billion.

Apple has six product lines so $14 billion multiple by six, we get $84 billion.

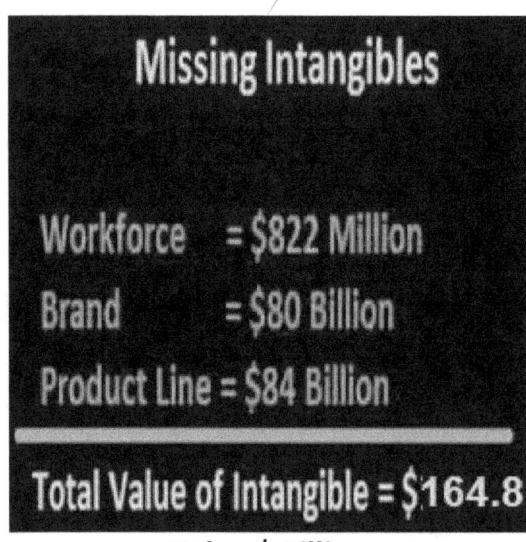

Value $ Billion

The Assets Valuation of Apple Inc Calculated

Calculating Asset Value

Value of Equity	$107 Billion
Adjustment in PPE +	$13.55 Billion
Good Will −	$0
Intangibles	
Product Line +	$84 Billion
Workforce +	$822 Million
Brands +	$80 Billion
Asset Value	$285 Billion

The Asset Value of Apple Inc is $285 Billion.

Earnings power value (EPV)

Earning power value: is the second aspect of the valuation of a business. Estimate of the corporate value based on the earnings power of a company's current sustainable distributable earnings. As it builds on today's earnings it's the second most reliable type of valuation. EPV estimates the enterprise value by dividing an earnings measure with the weighted average cost of capital (WACC, that is the cost of debt multiplied with the weight of debt in the company's financing, plus the cost of equity multiplied with the weight of equity financing). The earnings power value, or EPV, is a method which attempts to determine the underlying, or intrinsic, value of a given company's stock. The EPV strategy emphasizes the subject company's ability to earn cash in present terms, i.e. without factoring in the prospects of future earnings growth. A company's earnings power is its ability to generate cash, generally based on what a company has historically proven it can sustainably earn in conjunction with what the company is expected to earn in the future. The third component in determining a company's underlying value is the future growth of their earnings.

A business's ability to generate profit from conducting its operations. Earnings power is used to analyse stocks to assess whether the underlying company is worthy to investment. Possessing greater long-term earnings power is one indication that a stock may be a good investment.

As now we understood the assets value, now we will see how to value a company earning, value of earning in two ways in a company.

- *Sustainable earnings*
- *Growth earnings*

Sustainable earnings

Company's ability to generate a sustainable, and likely growing, stream of earnings that provide cash flow, this earning comes from the current operation of the business. The earning that remains stable form last 10 years and we can trust the earning for long team investing.

Growth Earnings

An earning is when a company need to infuse additional capital in their current operation to generate additional earning; a company can invest in same operation for the growth or do acquisitions.

Earning generates in the company in using both the earning Sustainable earnings and Growth earnings, for

EPV we need to follow Sustainable earnings in our valuation.

Let's understand the income statement, Revenue minus cost of goods sold minus operating expenses minus depreciation charges we get operating profit.

Revenues
- **Cost of goods sold (COGS)**
- **Operating expenses**
  - Wages
  - Marketing expenses
  - R&D expenses
- **Depreciation and amortization charges**
  - ± Over/under depreciation charges
  - +Expenses related to growth
  - ± Extraordinary items
= **Operating profit**

Revenue

In accounting, revenue is the income that a business has from its normal business activities, usually from the sale of goods and services to customers. Revenue is also referred to as sales or turnover. Some companies receive revenue from interest, royalties, or other fees.

Cost of goods sold

Cost of goods sold (COGS) refers to the direct costs of producing the goods sold by a company. This amount includes the cost of the materials and labor directly used to create the good. It excludes indirect expenses, such as distribution costs and sales force costs.

Operating expenses

Are those expenditures that a business incurs to engage in activities not directly associated with the production of goods or services? These expenditures are the same as selling, general and administrative expenses, research and development.

Depreciation and Amortization

Depreciation refers to the reduction in the cost of the tangible fixed assets over its lifespan which is proportionate to the use of the asset in that specific year. The example of tangible assets which are depreciated is the plant, equipment, machinery, building, and furniture. Depreciation of tangible assets can be done by using either a straight-line method or an accelerated depreciation method. Amortization refers to the reduction in the cost of the intangible assets over its lifespan. The examples of intangible assets which are amortized are patents, trademarks, lease rental agreements, concession rights, brand value, etc. Amortization of the intangible assets is mostly done using the straight-line method.

Company can take the depreciation charges, but in case of company take high depreciation charges than there will be low in earnings same applicable if company take low depreciation charges than earning will increase.

In order to know right sustainable earning, we need to compare depreciation with maintains caplex. Capital expenditure or capital expense is the money an organization or corporate entity spends to buy, maintains, or improves its fixed assets, such as buildings, vehicles, equipment, or land.

Depreciation & Maintenance Capital Expenditure

```
Adjustment

+ Depreciation charges
- Maintenance capex
+ Expense related to growth
+ Extraordinary items
```

Case A

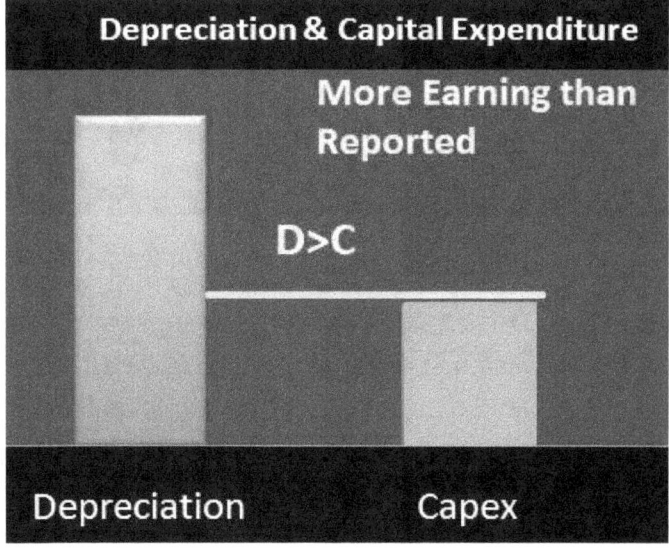

In Case A Company showing more depreciation to reduce the sustainable earning, but the actual earning is more than. Company have showing less in earning due to they have increase the depreciation.

Case B

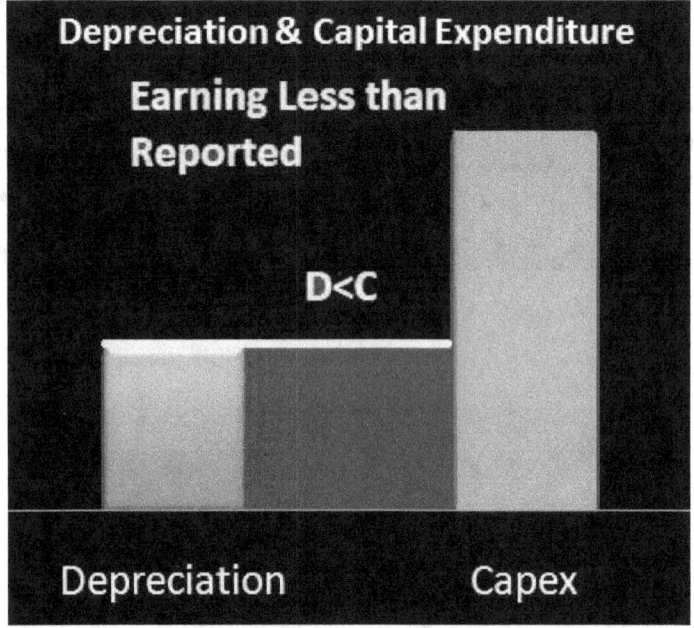

In the Case B company underreporting depreciation charges, in this case company have less earning, but to show rosy figure they reduce the depreciation charges to increase the sustainable earning.

Operating Profit

In accounting and finance, earnings before interest and taxes are a measure of a firm's profit that includes all incomes and expenses except interest expenses and income tax expenses.

After the entire deduction will be come up with the sustainable earning.

Calculation of Earning Power Value of Apple Inc

Income Statement

	Years ended		
	September 29, 2018	September 30, 2017	September 24, 2016
Net sales	$ 265,595	$ 229,234	$ 215,639
Cost of sales	163,756	141,048	131,376
Gross margin	101,839	88,186	84,263
Operating expenses:			
Research and development	14,236	11,581	10,045
Selling, general and administrative	16,705	15,261	14,194
Total operating expenses	30,941	26,842	24,239
Operating income	70,898	61,344	60,024
Other income/(expense), net	2,005	2,745	1,348
Income before provision for income taxes	72,903	64,089	61,372
Provision for income taxes	13,372	15,738	15,685
Net income	$ 59,531	$ 48,351	$ 45,687

Let start the calculation of Apple Inc Earning Power Value, in income statement we can see the net sale of apple in fiscal year 2018 is $265 billion, and the cost of goods is $163 billion, with the gross profit is $101 billion, Operating expenses include R&D and S, G&A, where R&D is $14 billion and Selling which include the marketing and advertising expenses , as apple don't disclose the marketing expenses ,and other operation expenses is $16.7 billion .

The total Operation expenses were $30.9 billion and operating income is $70.8 billion.

The Operating Margin of Apple

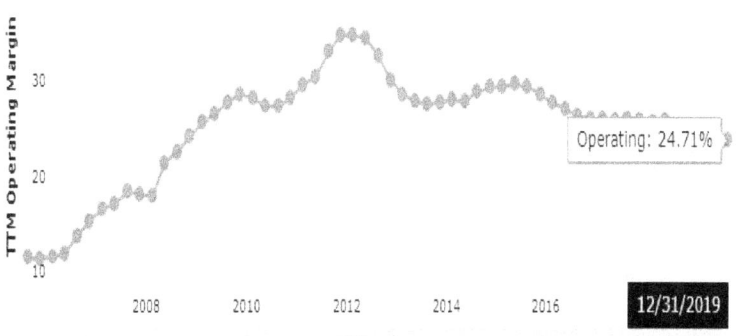

Apple Inc Operating Margin

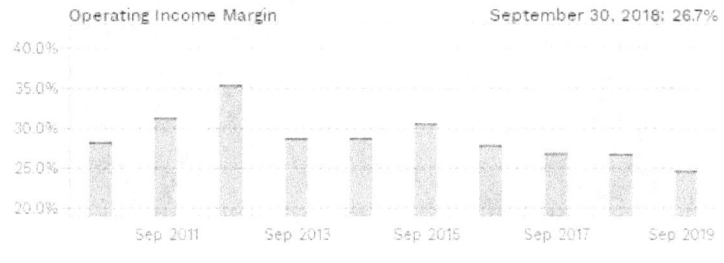

Apple Inc Operating Margin

The following section summarizes insights on Apple Inc.'s Operating Income Margin:

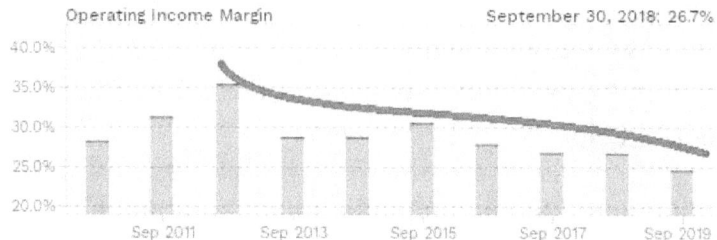

Apple Inc Operating Margin with Smooth Red Line

Operating Margin by Segment Geographical

	2016	2017	2018
Americas:	33%	32%	31%
Europe:	31%	30%	32%
Greater China:	39%	38%	38%
Japan:	42%	46%	44%
Rest Asia Pacific:	35%	35%	36%

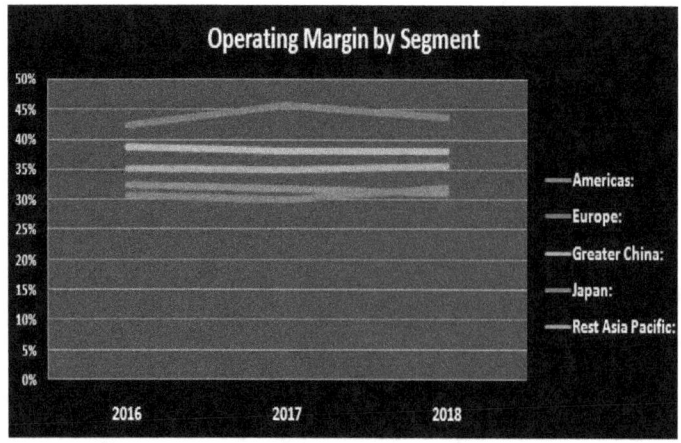

			2018	2017	2016
Americas:					
Net	sales		1,12,093	96,600	86,613
Operating	income		34,864	30,684	28,172
Operaing Margin			31%	32%	33%
Europe:					
Net	sales		62,420	54,938	49,952
Operating	income		19,955	16,514	15,348
Operaing Margin			32%	30%	31%
Greater China:					
Net	sales		51,942	44,764	48,492
Operating	income		19,742	17,032	18,835
Operaing Margin			38%	38%	39%
Japan:					
Net	sales		21,733	17,733	16,928
Operating	income		9,500	8,097	7,165
Operaing Margin			44%	46%	42%
Rest Asia Pacific:					
Net	sales		17,407	15,199	13,654
Operating	income		6,181	5,304	4,781
Operaing Margin			36%	35%	35%

Total Net Revenue		2,65,595	2,29,234	2,15,639
Total Operating Income		90,242	77,631	74,301
Operaing Margin		34%	34%	34%
Research and development expense		-14,236	-11,581	-10,045
Other corporate expenses, net		-5,108	-4,706	-4,232
Total operating income		70,898	61,344	60,024
Operaing Margin		27%	27%	28%

We take the average of seven year of operating margin as a smooth period, we will not consider the up and downs of the operating margin rather than we will see what is sustainable operating margin, if we see the operating margin of Apple in the year 2012 was 35 % but after 2016 there is a decrease in the operating margin, in this case we need to go deeper and find out what is the matter, the reason to decrease.

Apple Inc report sales and operating margin in different segment, if we notice the revenue and operating margin comes from the different segment such as from America, Europe, Greater China, Japan and Rest Asia Pacific. The collapsing operating margins are from two segment mainly America from 2016, margin 33% reduced to 31% and from Greater China from 2016, margin 39% reduced to 38%, the reason can be high competition with the other brands.

Other segment remains stable and increase in margin in Europe from 31% to 32%, and Rest of Asia Pacific from 35% to 36%.

We will take smooth number 26%

The Depreciation Adjustment of Apple

We will do adjustment in operating income and now look forward to depreciation.

Apple Inc Depreciation for last 3 years

Value	2018	2017	2016
Depreciation & Amortization	10.9	10.1	10.5
+ Capital Expenditure	13.3	12.4	12.7
+ Acquistions	0.721	0.329	0.297
Difference	3.1	2.6	2.5

We have made the adjustment from the Operating activities: mainly Depreciation and Amortization, we have taken the value from the cash flow statement of Apple Inc from fiscal year 2016, 2017,2018, and from the Investing activities: we have taken payments for acquisition of property, plant and equipment and payments made in connection with business acquisitions, net , to measure the measure of sustainable earnings , we need to calculate the difference of the depreciation , we have to check the depreciation presented by the company is stable or under reported or over reported .Whatever capex apple have done so far, all we need to calculate, as have taken last three years figure, you may take five year also, apple have done the acquisitions for all three years which is $721 Million in 2018, $329 Million in 2017 and $297 million in 2016, Apple has don't done big investment in acquisitions.

Apple have a stable number 3.1, 2.6 and 2.5, there is not much any changes, so we can trust apple, there no need for the further investigation.

Apple Inc WACC compare with industry

Going forward in the valuation of the EPV, we should consider the EPV estimates the enterprise value by dividing an earnings measure with the weighted average cost of capital (WACC, that is the cost of debt multiplied with the weight of debt in the company's financing, plus the cost of equity multiplied with the weight of equity financing). A high weighted average cost of capital, or WACC, is typically a signal of the higher risk associated with a firm's operations. Investors tend to require an additional return to neutralize the additional risk.

A company's WACC can be used to estimate the expected costs for all of its financing. This includes payments made on debt obligations (cost of debt financing), and the required rate of return demanded by ownership (or cost of equity financing) Value investors might also be concerned if a company's WACC is higher than its actual return. This is an indication the company is losing value, and there are probably more efficient returns available elsewhere in the market.

As we compare the WACC with the other company and in the same industry.

The Current Apple Inc WACC is 6.98%.

Competitive Comparison Data

Company	Market Cap (M)	WACC %
Apple Inc	$ 1,237,385.74	6.98
Samsung Electronics Co Ltd	$ 281,494.06	8.13
China Electronics Holding...	$ 124,978.90	0.00
Sony Corp	$ 79,045.27	5.10
Midea Group Co Ltd	$ 49,458.01	6.22
Gree Electric Appliances I...	$ 46,513.65	8.56
Xiaomi Corp	$ 32,211.72	0.00
Kyocera Corp	$ 20,322.54	7.42
Panasonic Corp	$ 17,162.22	4.75
Haier Smart Home Co Ltd	$ 13,819.02	7.64

Calculation of the Earning Power Value of Apple Inc to the Operating Business

Earning Power Value of Apple Inc
$ Billion

	Particulars	2018	Smoothed
	1 Revenue	265.6	
	2 Operating Margin %	26.7%	
1 X 2	3 Operating Income	70.9	
	4 Adjustments		
	5 Over/under Depreciation	0	
	6 Growth Expense	0	
3+5+6	7 Adjusted Income	70.9	
	8 Taxes %	18.3%	
7-(7 X 8)	9 Sustainable NOPAT	57.9	
	10 WACC %	7%	
9/10	11 EPV Operating Business	827.0	
	12 Non-Operational Cash	25.9	
	13 Debt	93.7	
11+12-13	14 EPV Equity	759.2	

If you see there is smooth number not shows and we need to calculate the smooth sustainable number, currently we have the number from the fiscal year 2018, we get the smooth number, we need to take the average of five to seven years, doing the average we may see the different number in different years, some years up and some year down, that the reason we will not be taking only one current year, we will take the average, now let see each particular one by one.

Revenue

In accounting, revenue is the income that a business has from its normal business activities, usually from the sale of goods and services to customers. Revenue is also referred to as sales or turnover. Some companies receive revenue from interest, royalties, or other fees. Revenue may refer to business income in general, or it may refer to the amount, in a monetary unit, earned during a period of time, as in "Last year, Profits or net income generally imply total revenue minus total expenses in a given period. In accounting, in the balance statement it is a subsection of the Equity section and revenue increases equity, it is often referred to as the "top line" due to its position on the income statement at the very top. This is to be contrasted with the "bottom line" which denotes net income (gross revenues minus total expenses).

Let look at the Apple Inc Revenue for last Seven years.

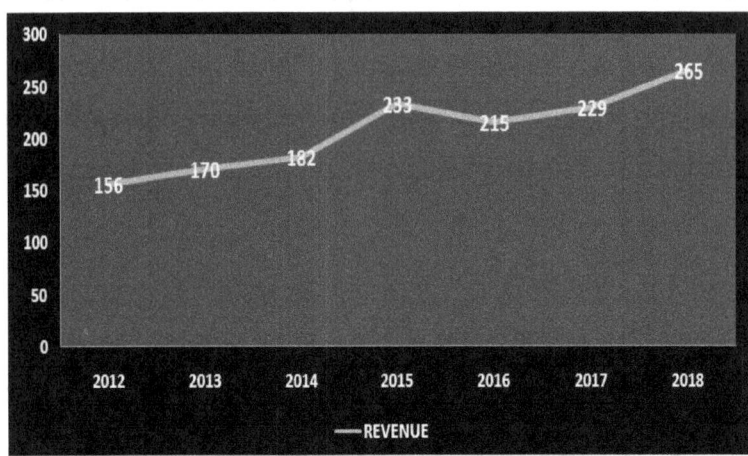

Apple Inc Revenue Last 7 Years

We can take smooth number $ 235 Billion.

Operating Margin

The operating margin measures how much profit a company makes on a dollar of sales, after paying for variable costs of production, such as wages and raw materials, but before paying interest or tax. It is calculated by dividing a company's operating profit by its net sales.

Operating Margin= Revenue / Operating Earnings

In business, operating margin—also known as operating income margin, operating profit margin, EBIT margin and return on sales (ROS). It is a measurement of what proportion of a company's revenue is left over, before taxes and other indirect costs (such as rent, bonus, interest, etc.), after paying for variable costs of production as wages, raw materials, etc. A good operating margin is needed for a company to be able to pay for its fixed costs, such as interest on debt. A higher operating margin means that the company has less financial risk.

We have already calculated the operating margin so will take smooth number 26%

Operating Income

Going forward we just need to multiply revenue to operating margin to get operating profit.

Adjustments

As we have already discussed the impact of the Over/under Depreciation and Growth Expense, Apple Inc take they not done any issue so that they are talking right number, so we will leave as it is to zero.

Adjusted Income

If we would have found any changes in the Over/under Depreciation and Growth Expense then we have to add to the operating income.

Taxes %

Corporate tax is imposed in the United States at the federal, most state, and some local levels on the income of entities treated for tax purposes as corporations. Since January 1, 2018, the nominal federal corporate tax rate in the United States of America is a flat 21% due to the passage of the Tax Cuts and Jobs Act of 2017. State and local taxes and rules vary by jurisdiction, though many are based on federal concepts and definitions. Taxable income may differ from book income both as to timing of income and tax deductions and as to what is taxable. The corporate

Alternative Minimum Tax was also eliminated by the 2017 reform, but some states have alternative taxes. Like individuals, corporations must file tax returns every year. They must make quarterly estimated tax payments. Groups of corporations controlled by the same owners may file a consolidated return.

We will change tax, for smooth number

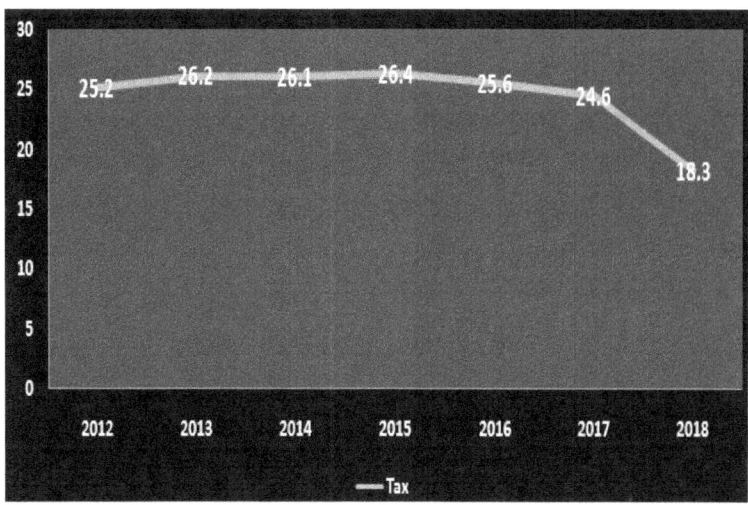

The Smooth Number for Tax will be 21 %

Sustainable NOPAT

There will be changes in the sustainable NOPAT as; there is a change in the Tax structure.

WACC %

As we have already calculated the cost of capital, for smooth number we will take same 6.98%

EPV Operating Business

When we will do changes in the all the above particulars like revenue, operating margin, change in operating profit, doing adjustment of deprecation, change in tax structure and using current cost of capital then we will get the sustainable Earning Power value, after adjusting all the number.

Non-Operational Cash

Cash and cash equivalents, you will find in the current assets, we will add the cash to the earning power value, to get the value with cash, as cash is liquid and are the at current cost so we will consider the cash also.

Debt

From the liabilities we will take long term debts and will deduct from the earning power value plus ad cash and minus the debts to get the Earning Power Value of Apple Inc.

Earning Power Value of Apple Inc

$ Billion

	Particulars	2018	Smoothed
	1 Revenue	265.6	235
	2 Operating Margin %	26.7%	26%
1 X 2	3 Operating Income	70.9	61.1
	4 Adjustments		
	5 Over/under Depreciation	0	0
	6 Growth Expense	0	0
3+5+6	7 Adjusted Income	70.9	61.1
	8 Taxes %	18.3%	21%
7-(7 X 8)	9 Sustainable NOPAT	57.9	48.3
	10 WACC %	7%	6.98%
9/10	11 EPV Operating Business	827.0	691.5
	12 Non-Operational Cash	25.9	25.9
	13 Debt	93.7	93.7
11+12-13	14 EPV Equity	759.2	623.7

Earning Power Value of Operating Business

We have got the Earning Power Value at current 2018 is $ 759.2 billion and when we use the smooth number it is $ 623 billion.

Now we will move forward to check can apple create value, apple enjoy barrier to entry and have competitive advantage in the industry, apple management performance to use their asset to generate the earning for the company.

We will check by the number, what the assets value of apple is and what the earning value is.

Apple Inc
Case C

$ 623 Billion

$285 billion
AV < EPV

Competative Advantage.
Barrier to Entry.
Efficent Management.

Asset value (AV)   Earnings power value (EPV)

Apple is in Case C; the company have Asset value of $285 Billion less than the Earning Power Value $ 623 Billion.

Competitive Advantage Apple

- Brand equity – customer are ready to pay the price to buy the iPhone of apple, apple can raise the price.

- Company enjoys competitive advantage with high market share in their segment.

- Barriers to entry, for a competitor it is not easy to replace apple because, to setup a company like apple, it will require huge investment and it will be a question, will it survive in the market.

- The management of apple use the asset properly to generate the high earning compare to assets.

- Apple EV < EPV

- Apple enjoy high margin.

- Apple operates in different country and performs well in each segment.

Apple AV, EPV and MV

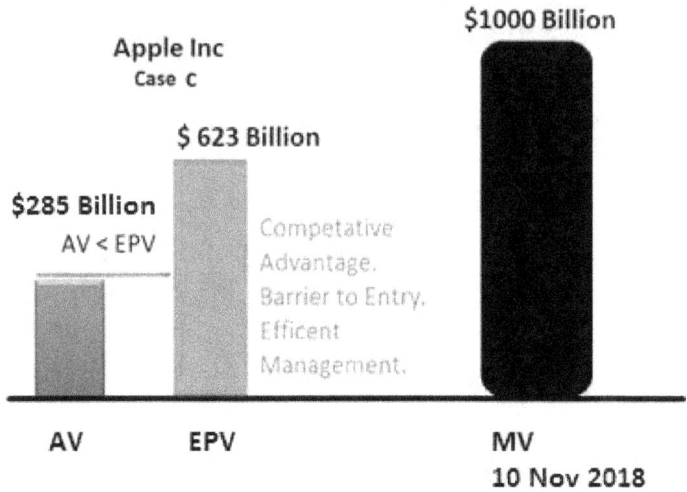

- AV = $ 285 Billon
- EPV =$ 623 Billion
- MV =$ $1000 Billion

Currently we don't have Margin of Safety, can still we buy? Let go ahead.

The legendary value investor Warren Buffett is holding this company share with the highest allocation in their portfolio. He bought the share in Sep 2018 for $225 and even he bought the shares at March 2018 at $185.

12

EV/EBITDA vs. EV/GROSS PROFIT

When we find the growth company, where EPV is less than the MV, where there is no margin of safety, for the growth company generally valuation is high so, we cannot able to understand whether to buy it or not.

We don't get the clear picture when we will use the EV/EBIDTA, so we need to use the other ratio EV/Gross Profit, there is a growth in Apple so even, and a lot of that growth has been expense. If we compare with Samsung to find out how expensive is Apple, let see the illustration to find out Apple and Samsung EV/EBIDTA and EV /Gross.

APPLE EV/EBIDTA AND EV/GROSS PROFIT RATIO

Year	Gross Profit	EV	EV/GP	EV/EBIDTA
2015	93.6	688	7.3	7.18
2016	84.2	636	7.6	8.58
2017	88.18	927	10.5	11.79
2018	101.8	1005	9.9	9.12
2019	98.3	1113	11.3	15.82

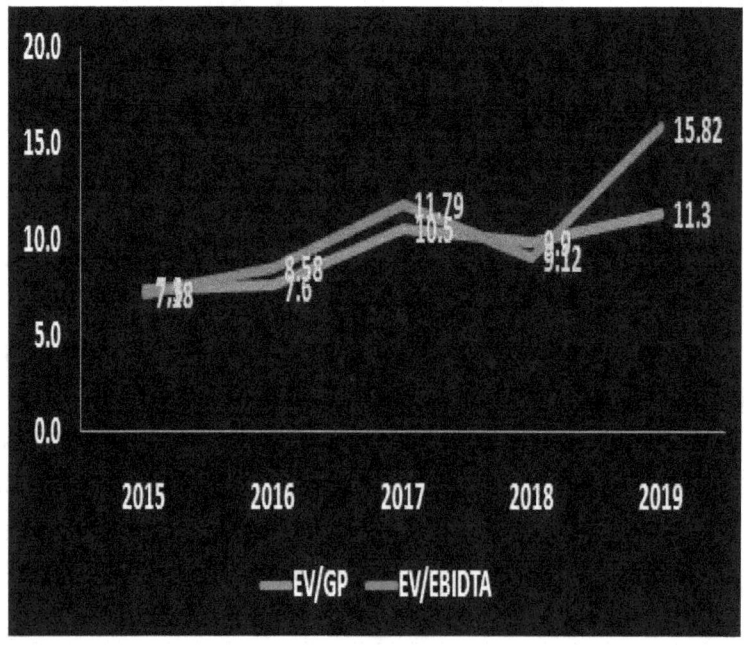

Apple

SAMSUNG EV/EBIDTA AND EV/GROSS PROFIT RATIO

Year	Gross Profit	EV	EV/GP	EV/EBIDTA
2015	66	105	1.6	2.76
2016	69	119	1.7	3.38
2017	102	258	2.5	3.67
2018	99	230	2.3	2.09
2019	71	194	2.7	4.13

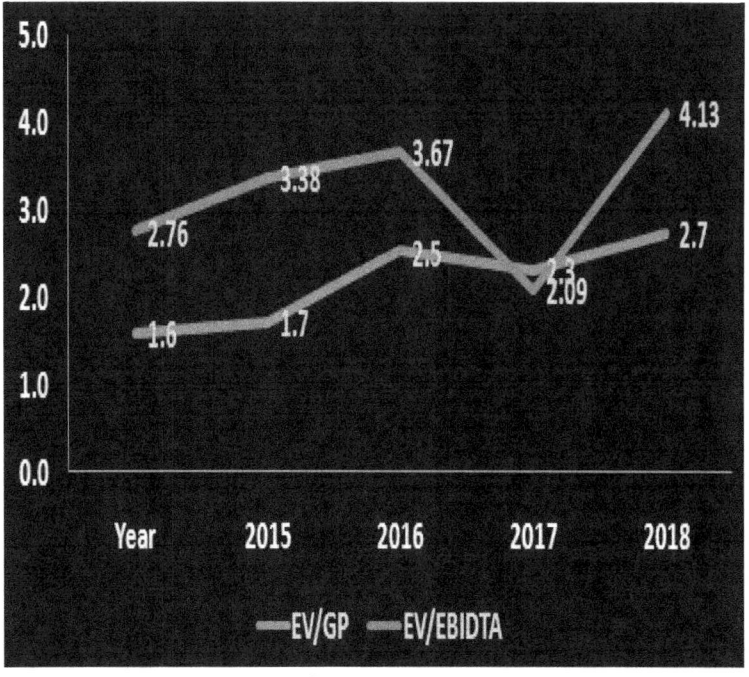

Samsung

Compare EV/EBIDTA

Year	Samsung	Apple
2015	2.76	7.18
2016	3.38	8.58
2017	3.67	11.79
2018	2.09	9.12
2019	4.13	15.82

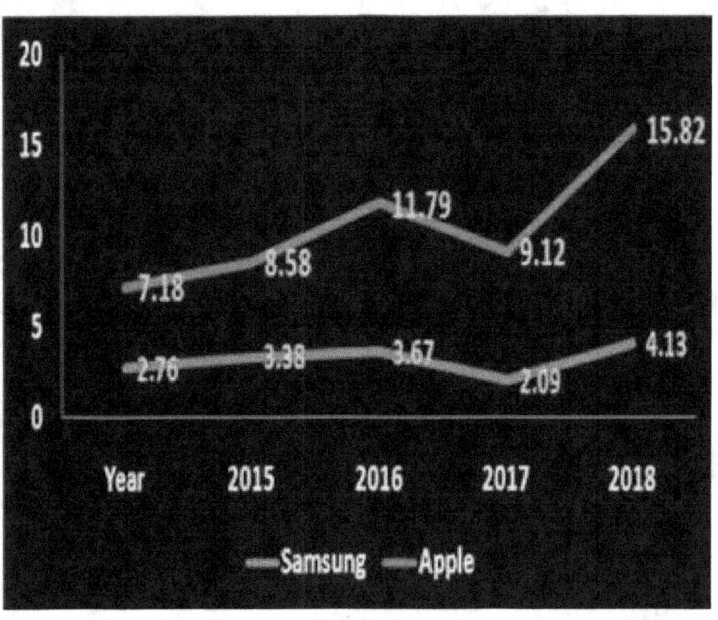

There is a difference in the EV/EBIDTA as in 2018 Samsung ratio was 4.13 compare with Apple 15.82, it looks like Apple stock is very expensive, might we buy Samsung, but Samsung Revenue growth is 3% CAGR compare with Apple is 5.55% CAGR, Apple is Growing faster than Samsung, so the valuation of Apple is expensive, how we will decide to buy Apple stock, we will understand in revenue growth and EV/GP.

Compare Revenue Growth

Year	Samsung	Apple
3-Year Average	4.5%	6.5%
5-Year Average	2.2%	7.3%
10-Year Average	5.4%	21.3%

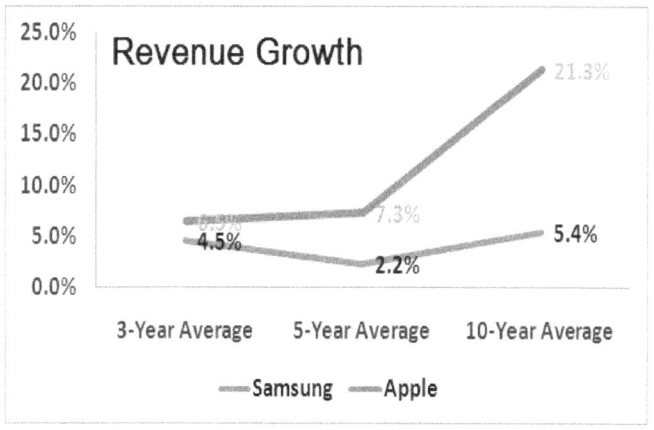

The revenue growth of both the company is different as Apple is growing at 21% for ten years compare with the Samsung is only 5.4%, there is ocean of difference, therefore apple stock needs to be expensive, and market value higher than Samsung, in the Smartphone industry apple is only player that is earning more than 80 % margin, compare with Samsung only 17 % margin.

Compare EV/GROSS PROFIT RATIO

Year	Samsung	Apple
2015	1.6	7.3
2016	1.7	7.6
2017	2.5	10.5
2018	2.3	9.9
2019	2.7	11.3

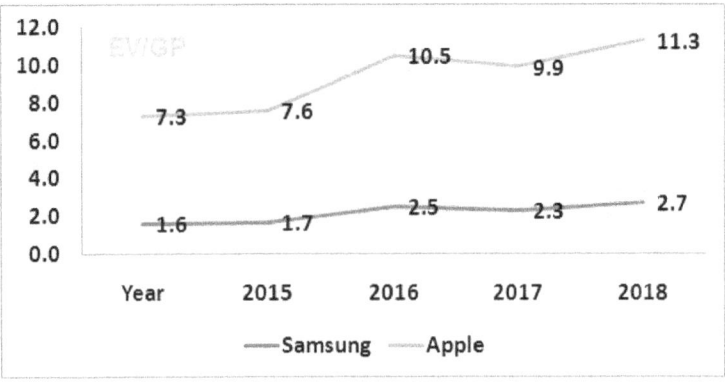

If we compare EV/GP, we can see there is not much difference between Samsung and Apple as we company with EV/EBIDTA.

We can use this Ratio EV/GP to buy Apple at this price, if we brought apple at $200 as on October 2018 and after one-year 2019 stock was trading at $332 per share, with the profit of $132 and gain of 66% return in one year.

This is one of the approach value investors do in growing company.

13

Franchise Value

- Value only when there is a franchise value such as barrier to entry.

- Company must have competitive advantage.

- Have deep moat.

- Barrier to entry should be sustainable.

- Company enjoys customer captivity.

- When you get a company with sustainable barrier to entry, you can do your valuation and buy the stock.

- When you buy a stock below the intrinsic value then you are getting growth for free.

- If company have barrier to entry competitive advantage and if you but the stock at valuation of Earning Power Value, then your future earning to create wealth in the investment is free.

Strategic Analysis

Now to calculate the franchise value before we calculate the value, we need to ask, are there barriers to entry, now new company can enter the market, company enjoy brands value, if we found that the assets value is more than the earning power value and there is no growth in the company, we will not explore the franchise value.

Because barriers to entry protect incumbent firms and restrict competition in a market, they can contribute to distortionary prices and are therefore most important when discussing antitrust policy. Barriers to entry often cause or aid the existence of monopolies or give companies market power.

Barriers to entry are the economic term describing the existence of high start-up costs or other obstacles that prevent new competitors from easily entering an industry or area of business. Barriers to entry benefit existing firms because they protect their revenues and profits.

Common barriers to entry include special tax benefits to existing firms, patents, customer loyalty, and high customer switching costs. Others include the need for new firms to obtain proper licenses or regulatory clearance before operation.

If company earning power is more than the assets value and company enjoy the barrier to entry, then we will move forward to calculate franchise value.

Let understand what is barrier to entry? And what not is a barrier to entry?

Barrier to entry

Supply Based
- **Patents**
- **Regulatory Licenses**
- **Cost advantage/Economic of Scale**

Demand Based
- **Network Switching Cost**
- **Habits**
- **Search**

Not a Barrier to Entry

- **Brands Based**
- **First Mover advantage**

Barrier to entry

Supply Based

Supply Based	
Barriers to Entry	Example
Intangible assets	
Patents	Coca cola, Apple.
Regulatory Licenses	Airbus, Johnson & Johnson.
Cost advantage/Economic of Scale	Walmart, Costco, Dollar General

Company have power to control the customer buying power that include the pricing of the product, in the supply-based barrier to entry company have patents, A patent is a form of intellectual property that gives its owner the legal right to exclude others from making, using, selling and importing an invention for a limited period of years, in exchange for publishing an enabling public disclosure of the invention. In most countries patent rights fall under civil law and the patent holder needs to sue someone infringing the patent in order to enforce his or her rights. In some industries patents are an essential form of competitive advantage.

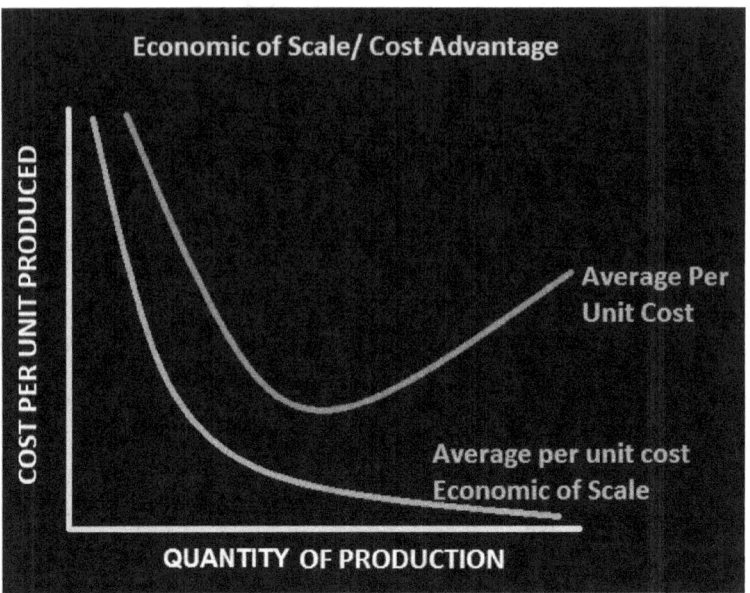

Company produces a product which have a cost per unit, if you see red line, it shows that if there is not barrier to entry then average cost to produce the product will increase, see the red line, its going upward trend compare with the blue line, the company produce more, the cost of each product will decrease and will help in increasing in the profit of the company.

Take Wal-Mart as they have so many stores in different country and have economic of scale, they sell at discounted price and customers are read to buy the product.

The company have a cost advantage and economic of scale, Economies of scale are cost advantages by companies when production becomes efficient. Companies can achieve economies of scale by increasing production and lowering costs. This happens because costs are spread over a larger number of goods. Costs can be both fixed and variable. The size of the business generally matters when it comes to economies of scale. The larger the business, the more the cost savings, such company like Wal-Mart, Costco.

Some company have unique access to develop the product like airbus, without the licence one cannot manufacture the product, and this licence is not for every company, the company which hold the licence have the property right to use it.

Demand Based

Demand Based	
Barriers to Entry	Example
Network Switching Cost	Microsoft, Facebook, Oracle, Visa & Mastercard.
Habits	Philip Morris
Search	Google

Microsoft was a master practitioner of "network effects," the straightforward precept in economics that the value of a product or service often goes up as more people use it. There is nothing new about the concept. A network effect (also called network externality or demand-side economies of scale) is the effect described in economics and business that an additional user of goods or services has on the value of that product to others. When a network effect is present, the value of a product or service increases according to the number of others using it, the network effect can create a bandwagon effect as the network becomes more valuable and more people join, resulting in a positive feedback loop.

Search is when customer don't have any option then to use the only one company product, just like Google has become so massive that we all use Google for any kind of search we want to do, even Facebook is a unique, there is no other Facebook where we can interact each other.

One of the important barriers to entry is habit, people don't mind paying more price of goods for their behavioural habit, because using the product they get the habit and it is not so easy to change, like cigarette is a habit and there is a company, Philip Morris.

Not a Barrier to Entry

Brands Based

Sometimes, one of the most successful companies face the biggest brand failures because of their strengths and past victories, which resulted in over-confidence and lulled them into complacency that they feel reluctant in trying new strategies and sometimes even don't even care about their current and prospective such as Nokia Brand Failure, This is the actual story of a brand which was once a market leader in the mobile phones industry, Nokia had a set of best hardware engineers but it overlooked the fact that the consumer preference was shifting from hardware to more of software. Hence, Apple (ios) and other companies like Samsung (Android) were able to crush Nokia and succeed in a comparatively short span of time.

Why Kodak Failed, Eastman believed in making photography available to everyone, by changing the way people took photographs. With the development of his new and innovative Kodak camera, Eastman made it possible for anyone interested in photography to take great pictures but they didn't understand that customer is switching to digital photography and smart phones capturing the market, as it turned out; digital cameras were not the biggest fish in the pond. Smartphones took the world by storm and digital cameras producers saw their sales quickly spiralling down. People went from printing pictures to storing them on digital devices or sharing them online on social media platforms. In 2012, when Kodak was filing for bankruptcy.

Branding work only when company restrict the supply of product as such Ferrari did in 2013, Ferrari started limiting its production to only 7,000 units per year; it continued to do so into 2014 before abandoning the cap shortly after as sales ramped up in new markets like China. Ferrari production is now uncapped, and we expect the sales numbers for 2018 to be quite high.

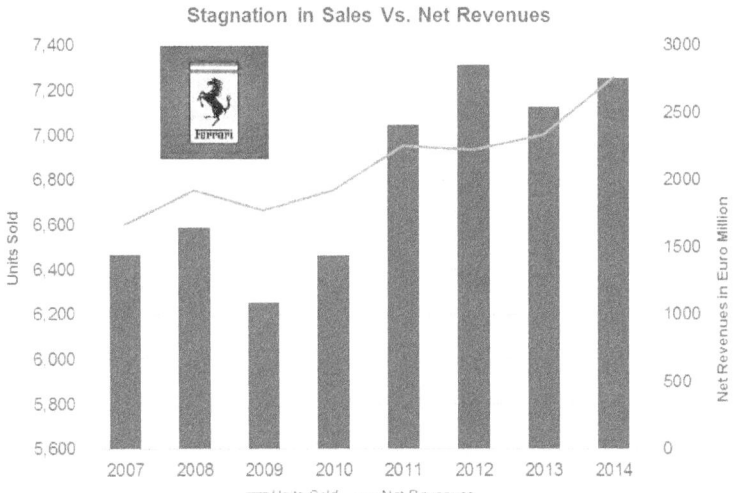

Ferrari sales figure with revenue

First Mover advantage

Nokia and Kodak failed even was the first mover but didn't last due to technological changes, company like blackberry messenger, every people once used to send text, photo etc but now WhatsApp Messenger, have replaced Blackberry.

Uber eat sell his business in India to a local Zamoto, Uber was having first mover advantage in India but didn't survived. AltaVista was a Web search engine established in 1995. It became one of the most-used early search engines, but lost ground to Google and was purchased by Yahoo! in 2003, which retained the brand, but based all AltaVista searches on its own search engine. On July 8, 2013, the service was shut down by Yahoo! and since then the domain has redirected to Yahoo!'s own search site.

Compaq (a portmanteau of Compatibility and Quality, occasionally referred to as CQ prior to its final logo) was a company founded in 1982 that developed, sold, and supported computers and related products and services. Compaq produced some of the first IBM PC compatible computers, being the first company to legally reverse the IBM Personal Computer. It rose to become the largest supplier of PC systems during the 1990s before being overtaken by HP in 2001. Struggling to keep up in the price wars against Dell, as well as with a risky acquisition of DEC, Compaq was acquired for US$25 billion by HP in 2002. The Compaq brand remained in use by HP for lower-end systems until 2013 when it was discontinued.

14

Competitive Advantage

Ways to measure the competitive advantage is by the size of the market, where company enjoy in the market, as we look at the market share of the company .In business, a competitive advantage is the attribute that allows an organization to outperform its competitors. A competitive advantage may include access to natural resources, such as high-grade ores or a low-cost power source, highly skilled labor, geographic location, high entry barriers, and access to new technology.

Competitive advantage is the leverage a business has over its competitors. This can be gained by offering clients better and greater value. Advertising products or services with lower prices or higher quality piques the interest of consumers. Target markets recognize these unique products or services. This is the reason behind brand loyalty, or why customers prefer one particular product or service over another.

Value proposition is important when understanding competitive advantage. If the value proposition is effective, that is, if the value proposition offers clients better and greater value, it can produce a competitive advantage in either the product or service.

Measuring the competitive advantage

First to know what is the size of the market in which company is operating. We need to look at the share of the company in overall of the industry.

$$\frac{\text{Revenue of the Company}}{\text{Total Revenue of the industry}}$$

- If the market shrinks or degrowth in the market, the competitive advantage of the company increases, the market share increase, company create more barrier to entry and enjoy competitive advantage in the industry.

- In case market increases and growth in the industry, the growth of the company will be less as there will be decline in the market share of the company. Growth in industry attract new competitors and they try to get the market share to survive.

Let see the example of the Apple in year 2018.

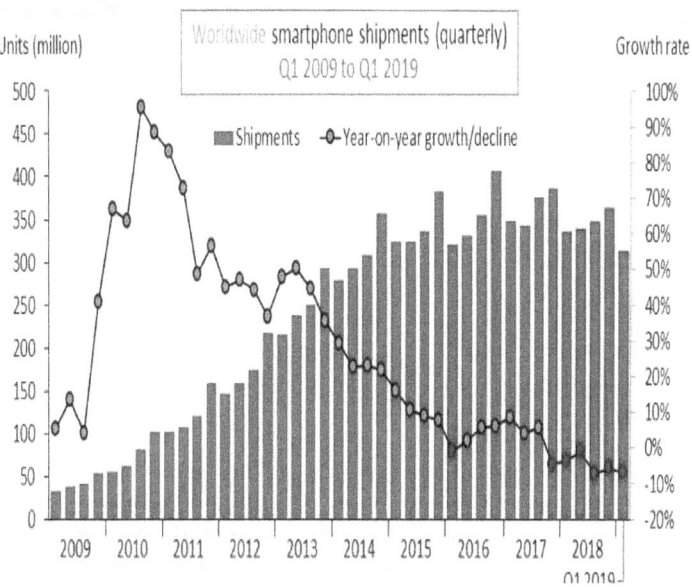

There is a degrowth, decline in the overall Smartphone industry, you can see stating of 2018, there is decline of -5%, this is a negative year for the Smartphone industry. There is decline in the shipment of Smartphone as we compare with the market share of apple at this time year 2018.

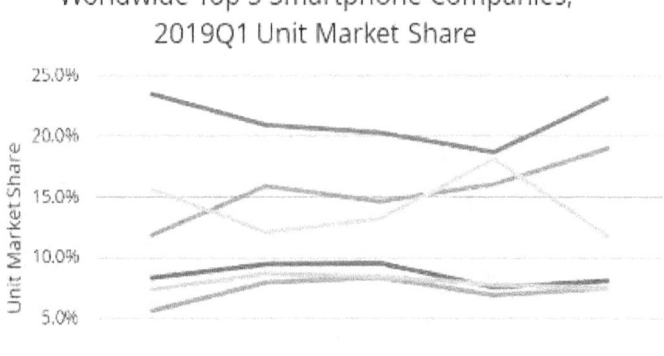

If you see the graph, there is an increase in the market share from 12% to 15 % but it could not sustain again reach to same level.

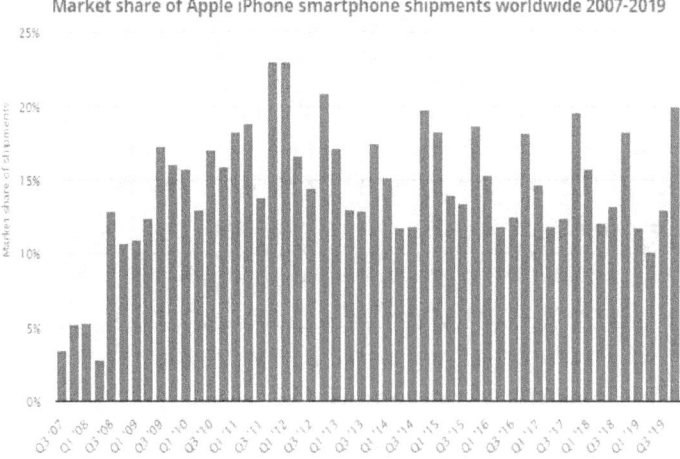

It is good to see a decline in industry and the company whose market share increase, indicate that company have the competitive advantage.

15

Three Step to Perform a Strategic Analysis

STEP 1

The Firm

- **Segment Inside the firm**
    - What does firm do?
    - Check revenue breakup?
    - Which market do they operate?

- **Trends inside the firm**
    - Which segment is growing?
    - Which segment is declining?
    - Growth by Synergy?
    - Organic business growth?

STEP 2

The Industry

- Each segment company with competitors?

- If company operate in different industry, then look for competitors in each segment?

- Trends in industry, free entrance to competitors, or restricted entry in the industry?

- Do they have barriers to entry and competitive advantage?

STEP 3

Value Chain

- The substitute's products interconnected with each other?

These are the three step to analyse the strategic performance of a company in three segments, the firm, which include the asking the questing what firm do, what is their revenue breakup in each segment, what is the operating margin in each segment, are margin increasing or there a decrease in margin, which segment, we find sales is increasing and to understand which all market company operate.

The second step is the industry , in this we will be understanding the industrial map , which is the segment company operate and which all bands they have , who are the competitors are in each brands , is there any barriers to entry , what kind of barrier to entry is there , its low , medium or high, who are the players in the market in local level as well as global level , suppose if we are analyses Wal-Mart, what is the average stock size ?, what is the creditors outstanding days across the retail industry ? .

The third is the value chain; here we will be looking in to interconnection of value as Wal-Mart sell retail product, so other manufactures are connected with Wal-Mart to sell their product, if there is effect in FMCG sector, what effect will be there in Wal-Mart.

The Firm

We need to dive deep in the firm and find out each product, segment they operate.

Revenue Breakup across each segment

Apple has changed a lot, company report in six segments:

- iPhone
- iPad
- Mac
- iPod
- Services
- Other Products

Fraction of Sales by Segment

Segment	2013	2014	2015	2016	2017	2018
iPhone	53%	56%	66%	63%	62%	63%
iPad	19%	17%	10%	10%	8%	7%
Mac	13%	13%	11%	11%	11%	10%
iPod	3%	1%				
Services	9%	10%	9%	11%	13%	7%
Other Products	3%	3%	4%	5%	6%	6%
Total	100%	100%	100%	100%	100%	100%

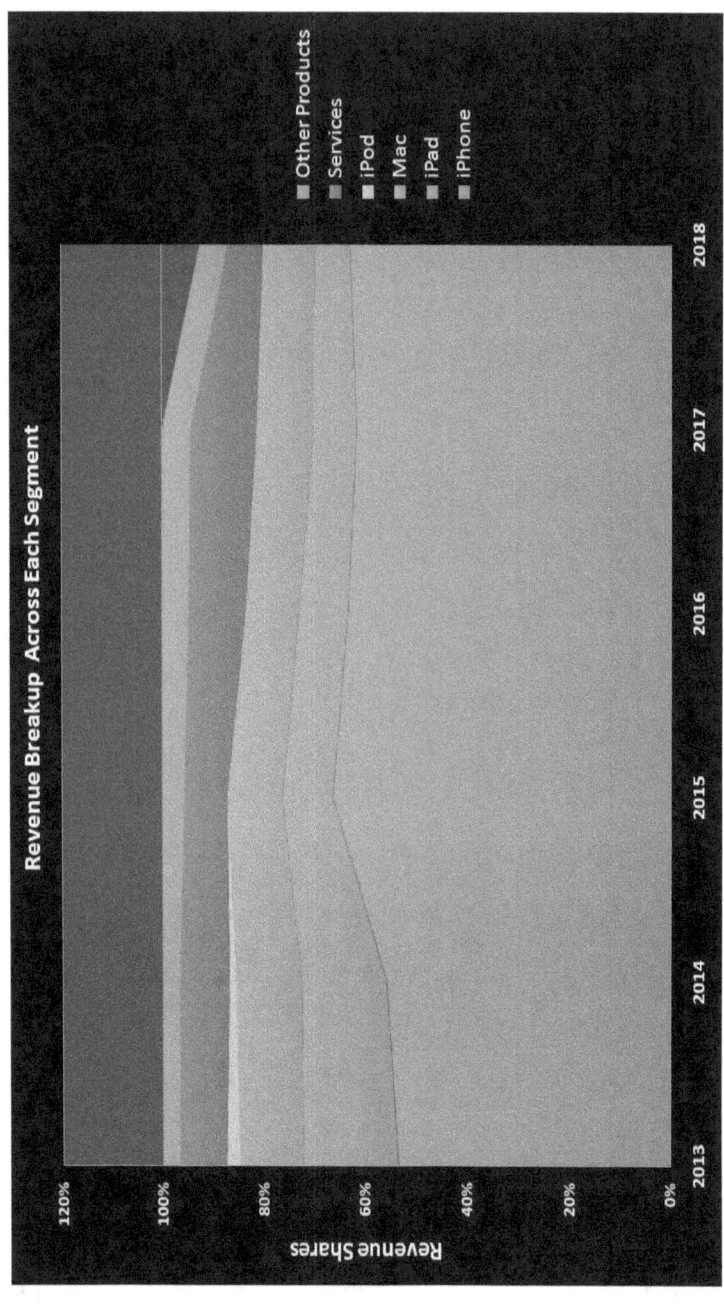

In this graph you have all the revenue contributing to the sales of the company, from 2013 to 2018, if you see in the graph 2013 and 2014 iPod sales was dropping and in 2015, there is no contribution of the iPod sale compare with iPhone contribute large shares in the revenue, 63%, there is an increase in sales of other products like Apple watch.

Apple was basically was a computer manufacturing but now Mac contributes only 10 % of the revenue, apple have changed a lot in 40 years. Apple was once used to be a computer company but currently it is a multi-branded company that sell Smartphone, watch, computer etc

Breakup across each segment, Industry and Competitors

Segment Wise Competitors in each Industry

Segment	Industry	Competitors
iPhone	SmartPhone	Samsung, Google, Huawei
iPad	Computer	Microsoft, Dell, Amazon Kindle
Mac	Computer	HP, Dell, Lenovo
Services	Music, Pay, Cloud	Microsoft, Paypal, Amazon
Other Products	smartwatches	Huawei, Garmin, Samsung

Apple is competing in each of the segment, like in Smartphone, there major competitors is Samsung and Huawei and Google, in the computer segment they have Microsoft, Dell and Lenovo, in iPad segment they have Amazon kindle, Microsoft and Dell. In the service they have three sub segments like music, pay and cloud service, each sub segment has different competitors like in music they have Microsoft, in pay, they have PayPal and in cloud they have Amazon as a competitor, last is the other products in which they sell apple watches, it's a smartwatch, here they have Samsung, Huawei and Garmin, understanding each segment if very important to do the strategic analyses.

Reporting Segment Wise 2012-2018

If you see 2014 product segment apple disclose is Desktops (a), Portables (b) ,Pod ,Other music related products and services (c) ,iPhone and related products and services (d) ,iPad and related products and ,services (e) ,Peripherals and other hardware (f) ,Software, service and other sales (g),if you see apple have changed the reporting of Desktops (a), Portables (b) to Mac and other product segment to iTunes, software and services (c) and Accessories (d) and in 2018 all the reporting segment have been changed to new format , we need to have clear picture in reporting of each segment in details , when we see this segment .

Reporting Segment Wise 2012-2018

2012	2013	2014	2015	2016	2017	2018
Desktops (a)	iPhone (b)	iPhone (b)	iPhone	iPhone	iPhone	iPhone
Portables (b)	iPad (b)	iPad (b)	iPad	iPad	iPad	iPad
iPod	Mac (b)	Mac (b)	Mac	Mac	Mac	Mac
Other music related products and services (c)	iPod (b)	iPod (b)	Services	Services	Services	Services
iPhone and related products and services (d)	iTunes, software and services (c)	iTunes, software and services (c)	Other Products	Other Products	Other Products	Other Products
iPad and related products and services (e)	Accessories (d)	Accessories (d)				
Peripherals and other hardware (f)						
Software, service and other sales (g)						

Segment by Revenue of Apple Inc

Fraction of Revenue by Segment

	FY 14	FY 15	FY 16	FY 17	FY 18
iPhone	101991	155041	136700	141319	166699
iPad	30283	23227	20628	19222	18805
Mac	24079	25471	22831	25850	25484
Services	18063	19909	24348	29980	37190
Other Products	8379	10067	11132	12863	17417
Total	182795	233715	215639	229234	265595

Value in $Million

- There is a good increase in the shipment of the iPhone and that is one of the best apple did, from 2014 with the sales of $101 billion increased to in 2018 were $166 billion .iPhone increase sale in four year is $66 billion, iPhone is a game changer for Apple company.

- There is a big degrowth in the in iPad sale in 2014 it was $30 billion and it shrink to $18 billion, more than 40 %, one of the product where apple lost around $12 billion.

- The sale of Mac in 2014 was $24 billion and after four years in 2018, the sales were $ 25 billion, not much changes, the sale of mac is sustainable. Earlier apple was known as a computer company but now due to massive growth in iPhone it has become a Smartphone company.

- There is a good growth in the apple services include like cloud service, apple pay, music, from $18 billion it has increased to $37 billion.

- Other product includes the apple watch, which is gaining market share in smart watches, from $8 billion to in 2018 is $ 17 billion, a 100 % growth, thanks to apple watch.

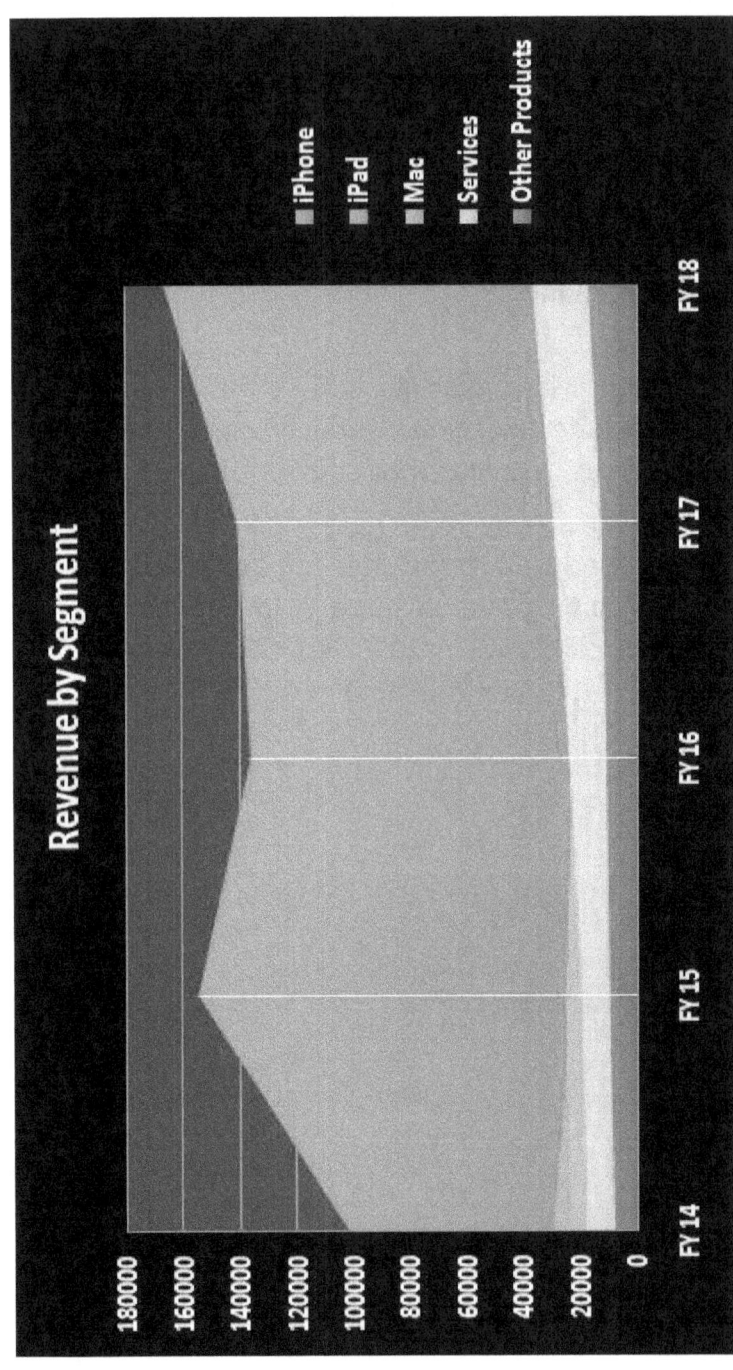

There are two more data we need to get but apple annual report doesn't have the data, apple doesn't provide.

- Apple Inc Operating Income of Each Product.
- Apple Inc Operating Margin Income of Each Product.

All the company don't share all this data, so you need to check individually when you analyse companies.

Reporting each unit Sale Wise 2015-2018

Reporting each unit Sale Wise 2015-2018					
	FY 14	FY 15	FY 16	FY 17	FY 18
iPhone	169219	231218	211884	216756	217722
iPad	67977	54856	45590	43753	43535
Mac	18906	20587	18484	19251	18209

- There is an increase in the sale of iPhone from 16912 unit sold have increased to 217722 unit million.
- Decrease sale of iPad and stability in mac .

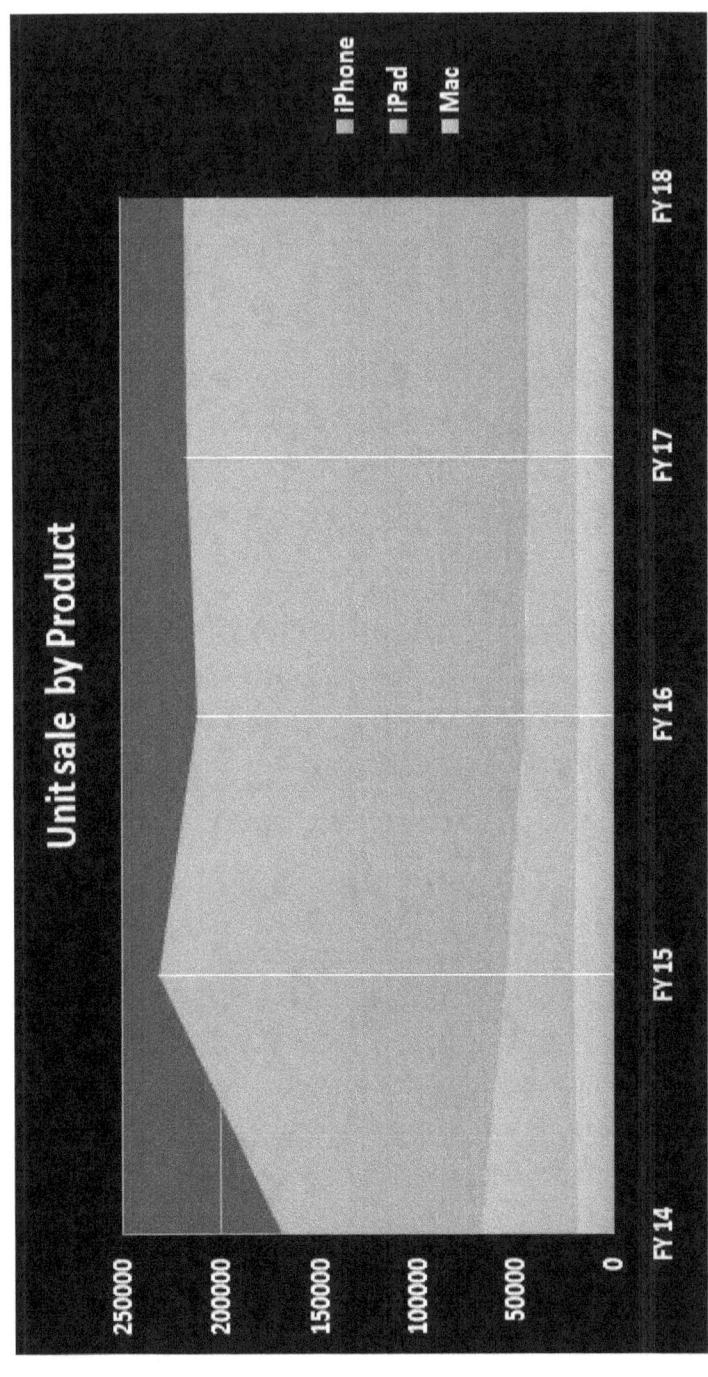

Ratio Margin of Income Statement

Fraction of Margin

	Mar-13	Mar-14	Mar-15	Mar-16	Mar-17	Mar-18
Gross margin	37.6%	38.6%	40.1%	39.1%	38.5%	38.3%
Operating Margin	29.2%	29.3%	31.0%	27.8%	26.8%	26.7%
PBT Margin	28.7%	28.7%	30.5%	27.8%	26.8%	26.7%
Net Margin	21.7%	21.6%	22.8%	21.2%	21.1%	22.4%

We need to check yearly the margin is stable, sinking or growing, for a competitive advantage company margins remain the same and some time it increases, as we see in the apple the gross margin from 37.6% to 40% and in 2018 is 38.3%, it shows that company have competitive advantage to maintain the price of the product.

Operating Margin has decreased due to research and development, well its ok, and net margin can be different time to time as there is a taxation issue, tax can be change in yearly basis, but still, we get the idea of stability.

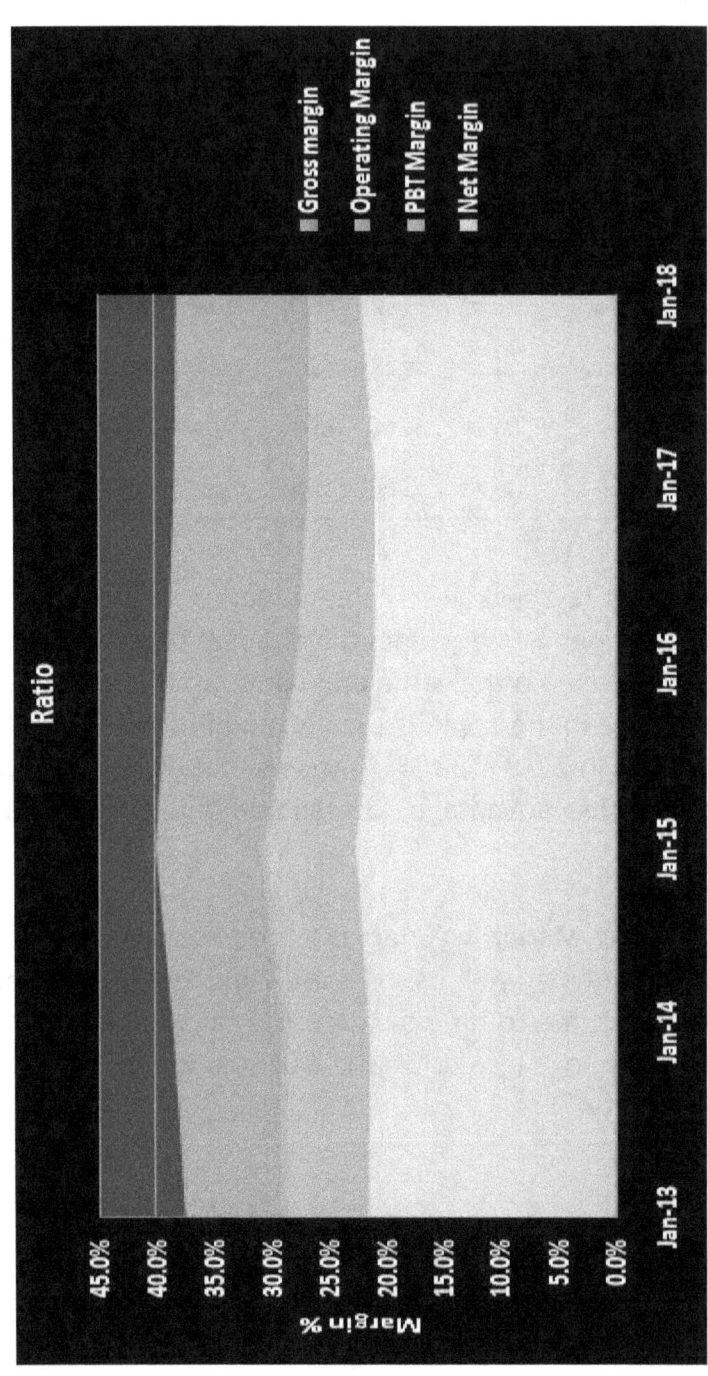

Apple Growing Organically or Acquisitions

List of Apple Inc Acquisitions

Year	Acquisitions	Price
2011	C3 Technologies	$267 million
2010	Quattro Wireless	$275 million
2008	P.A. Semi	$278 million
2012	AuthenTec	$356 million
2013	PrimeSense	$360 million
1997	NeXT	$404 million
2010	Siri	undisclosed

Apple is growing in both ways through the Organic business growth is related to the growth of natural systems and economies, as a dynamic organizational process, that for business expansion is marked by increased output, customer base expansion, or new product development, as opposed to mergers and acquisitions, which is inorganic growth and by acquisitions, apple is a acquisitions machine, company acquire lots of company.

The Industries

In the industries analysis we will check the each of the segment company operates in with the competitors, in that segment.

- Check the revenue and profit of each firm operating in the industry and company with the company you are analysing.

- Check which company is entering in the sector and which company are leaving the industry.

- The cost of increase in raw material or changes in tax, can be pass to the customer by increasing the price of the product, those company doesn't able to pass the cost and absorbed, then there is no barrier to entry.

- The company restricting the supply as we discussed example of Ferrari, they only manufacture 7000 unit of car, if customer want to but then they need to wait for the car.

- Use some other evidence from the market to understand what is happing in the industry.

Example Apple Inc.

Industry Map of Apple Inc		
Segment	Brands	Competitors
SmartPhone	iPhone	Samsung, Google, Huawei
Computer	iPad	Microsoft, Dell, Amazon Kindle
Computer	Mac	HP, Dell, Lenovo
Music	Services	Microsoft, Paypal, Amazon
smartwatches	Other Products	Huawei, Garmin, Samsung
Pay	Services	Paypal, Amazon Pay
Cloud	Services	Microsoft

Apple in each Segment with competitors, apple operates in different segment so they have competitors in each segment.

Profit value by Smartphone Company

Samsung, with just 17% of profit, in spite of growing 8.4% year-over-year in Q3, and selling between 20 to 30% of all mobile handsets on the planet.

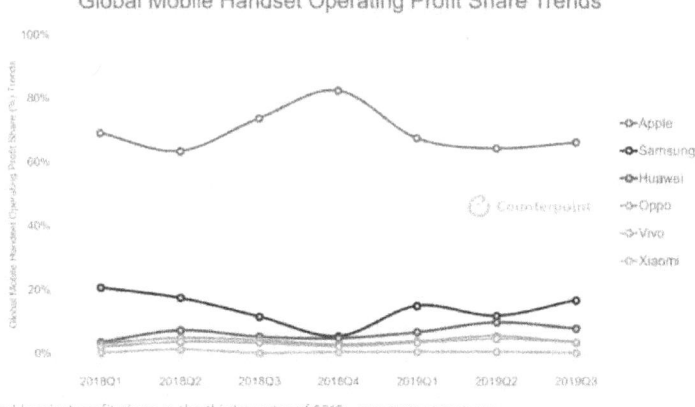

This graph state that no one make profit like apple in the Smartphone industry. Apple make around 75 % of profit from Smartphone, where Samsung sell more phone but only make 17 % of profit, look at this data there is a huge barrier to entry in the industry, only apple is making money and other are just there in the market.

Overall Performing Strategic Analyses

Overall Performing Strategic Analyses

Segment	Brands	Market	Barriers to entry	Competitors
		(Local vs. global)	(High/Medium/Low)	
Computer	Mac	GLOBAL	HIGH	Lenova,HP,Toshiba,Acer,Dell
Software	iTunes, Software and Services	GLOBAL	LOW	Oracle,Mcrosoft,Google
Consumer Electronic	iPhone	GLOBAL	MEDIUM	Samsung,Nokia, Amazon, Hauwai,Lenova
Music	iPod	GLOBAL	LOW	Xbox Music,Samsung
Pay	other Product	GLOBAL	LOW	Google Wallet

In this plot we can see the segment wise, brands, which market they operate, the competition in the market, local as well as global. Which product segment Apple have barrier to entry and if so, it is low, high or medium, and last we see who are the competitors in each segment.

In the plot we can get lots of information about the company product and the market and competitive advantage in each product.

Check the ROIC for the barriers to entry in the same industry.

Return on capital, or return on invested capital, is a ratio used in finance, valuation and accounting, as a measure of the profitability and value-creating potential of companies relative to the amount of capital invested by shareholders and other debt holders

Competitive Comparison Data

Company	Market Cap (M)	ROIC %
Apple Inc	$ 1,237,385.74	48.13
Samsung Electronics Co Ltd	$ 281,494.06	11.52
China Electronics Holding…	$ 124,978.90	0.00
Sony Corp	$ 79,052.62	18.09
Midea Group Co Ltd	$ 49,458.01	22.94
Gree Electric Appliances I…	$ 46,513.65	0.00
Xiaomi Corp	$ 32,211.72	0.00
Kyocera Corp	$ 20,324.43	5.05
Panasonic Corp	$ 17,163.81	12.00
Haier Smart Home Co Ltd	$ 13,819.02	18.48

Apple ROIC 48.13% it simply states that, apple have moat and enjoy competitive advantages in the industry as compare with Samsung is only having 11.52%.

Apple Competitive Advantage

Apple Segment Wise competative Advantages			
Product	Segment	Competative Advantages	Status
iPhone	SmartPhone	Strong	Growth
iPad	Computer	Low	Decline
Mac	Computer	Medium	Stable
Services	Music	Medium	Stable
Other Products	smartwatches	Strong	Growth
Services	Pay	Low	weak
Services	Cloud	Medium	Stable

- iPhone have a competitive advantage, because of its operating system, that only apple can manufacture and there is growth in the industry.
- iPad have low competitive advantage and it's in decline mode
- Mac is having medium competitive advantage and sales are stable.
- In services like apple music, they are having medium and stable.
- In other product like apple watch, they are having strong moats and growth.
- Service includes pay and cloud in this they have low and medium and weak and stable.

Growth Creates Value

Every company have to generate at least above the cost of capital in which they can fund them self, in this we will see how company create value and destroy value. How we will determine that a company is enjoy barrier to entry and have competitive advantage.

Growth Create Value

WACC 10%	Investment $1 Billion		
ROIC %	5%	10%	20%
Cost of Investment	$100 Million	$100 Million	$100 Million
Return	($50 Million)	$0 Million	$200 Million
Income Created	($50 Million)	$0 Million	$100 Million
Impact on Investment	Value Distroyed	No Value Created	Value Created
Status	NO Competative Advantage	Free Market	Competative Advantage

- Growth creates value only when the company return is above of cost of capital, company return on invested capital should be above the cost of capital.
- Return is very important for a company to be in the market, investment can be a successful investment when a company return is in higher side and to create value.

The example of the investment of $1 Billion state that how company create value and destroy the value.

- WACC is 10 % and Investment in Business is $1 Billion

- First case the ROIC return is 5%, the cost of investment is $1 Billion and company return are $50 Million, with the net loss of $50 Million, its mean $50 Million of capital is destroyed, company don't have the competitive advantage because its ROIC is below the cost of Capital.

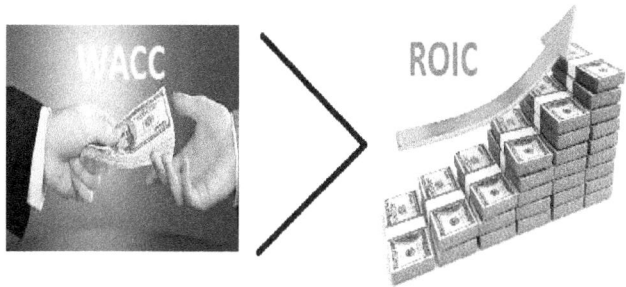

- Second case the ROIC return is 10%, the cost of investment is $1 Billion and company return are $100 Million, in this case neither value neither created nor destroyed, $000 Million of capital created, its ROIC is equal to the cost of Capital.

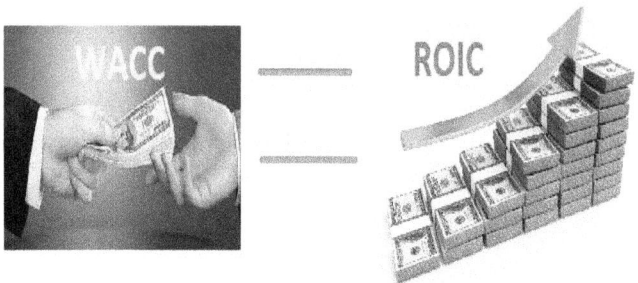

- First three the ROIC return is 20%, the cost of investment is $1 Billion and company return is $200 Million, with the net profit is $100 Million, its mean $100 Million of capital is created, company have the competitive advantage because its ROIC is above the cost of Capital.

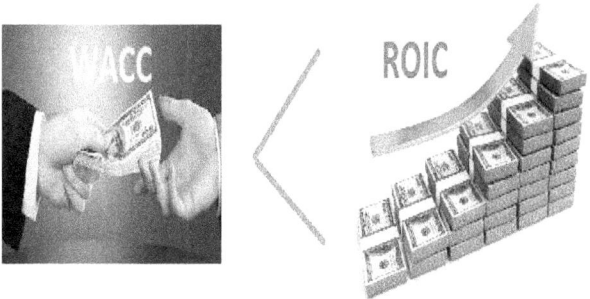

Rate of Growth & Earning

All the company are not fully funded only by equity; therefore, we need to calculate the enterprising value of the company, and there are ways find of growth a company create as follows:

- Growth Return

    This return comes when a company make a new investment, like acquiring a company for the growth as we have earlier come cross about the apple Inc. Apple Inc growth through the acquisition.

- Organic Growth

    An organic growth strategy seeks to maximize growth from within. There are many ways in which a company can increase sales internally in an organization. These strategies typically take the form of optimization, reallocation of resources, and new product offerings.
    Optimization of a business focuses on continuing to improve a business's processes to reduce costs and set appropriate pricing strategies for products or services. Reallocation of resources involves allocating funds and other materials to the production of best-performing products, while new product offerings seek to grow a business by introducing new goods and services that will add to profits and overall growth.

    Organic growth allows for business owners to maintain control of their company whereas a merger or acquisition would dilute or strip away their control. On the other hand, organic growth takes longer, as it is a slower process to acquire new customers and expand business with existing customers. A combination of both organic and inorganic growth is ideal for a company, as it diversifies the revenue base without relying solely on current operations to grow market share.

Calculation of Growth and Earning

- **Growth Return Calculation has two steps.**

   Step 1

   - Calculating Distribution Yield

   To calculation we need to check the cash flow statement, everything company distribute to the outside shareholders such as dividends ,share repurchase ,coupons and debts repayments.

   Step 2

   - Historical Earning Growth Rate

      We need to check average rate of growth of earnings and project that.

Calculating Distribution Yield of Apple Inc

Step 1

Calculate the Enterprise Value of Apple

EV of Apple		
Market Cap:		$1000 Billion
Long Term Debts :	+	$93.7 Billion
Cash :	-	$25.9 Billion
Enterprise Value		$1067.8 Billion

Apple Enterprise Value 2018 is $1067.8 Billion

Now Calculate the Distribution Yield, that company distribute to the shareholders and debts holders, as per Cash Flow statement and Income Statement.

Distribution Yield

Income Statement	Cash Flow Statement
+ Interest Expense :	Financing activities:
	Devidends:
	Share Repurchase : +
	Net Borrowing : +
	Other : +

- From income statement we will get the interest expenses.

- From cash flow statement we go to financing activities from there we will get dividends, shares repurchase, net borrowing and other expenses.

Distribution		
Devidends:		$13.7 Billion
Share Repurchase :	+	$72.7 Billion
Interest Expense :	+	$2 Billion
Net Borrowing :	+	$6.5 Billion
Other :	+	$2.6 Billion
Distribution		$97.5 Billion

Distribution Yield of Apple Inc

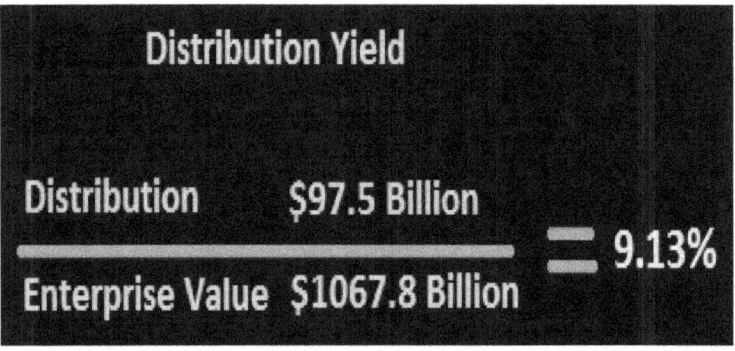

The Distribution Yield of Apple Inc calculated is 9.13%

Calculation Historical Earning Growth Rate

In this method we will see check the revenue for five to ten years, changes in the revenue, it there is an increase in revenue we will make the average or else if there is decrease in the revenue , we will take the zero value as a growth rate .

To calculate, we need to find three ratio growths

- Revenue growth, we will check the revenue for last five to ten years to find out the growth.

- EBIT, check the growth of Earning Before Interest and Tax, there is any improvement in EBIT, then revenue, suppose revenue has decline and what about the EBIT, it is important ratio to know pure growth.

- Properties, Plant & Equipment, what is PPE in the different cycle of yearly revenue, are company buying PPE to increase revenue.

Let see the example of Apple Inc

Apple Revenue 2012-2018

Apple Revenue Growth

YEAR	REVENUE	RETURN
2012	156	
2013	170	9.0%
2014	182	7.1%
2015	233	28.0%
2016	215	-7.7%
2017	229	6.5%
2018	265	15.7%
	5.44%	9.76%
CAGR RETURN	5.44%	
AVERAGE RETUN	9.76%	

Apple EBIT 2012-2018

Apple EBIT Margin Growth

YEAR	Margin	RETURN
2012	35.3	
2013	28.7	-18.7%
2014	28.7	0.0%
2015	30.5	6.3%
2016	27.8	-8.9%
2017	26.8	-3.6%
2018	26.7	-0.4%
	-2.75%	-4.21%
CAGR RETURN	-2.75%	
AVERAGE	-4.21%	

Apple PPE Growth 2012-2018

YEAR	PPE	RETURN
2012	15.4	
2013	16.5	7.1%
2014	20.6	24.8%
2015	22.4	8.7%
2016	27	20.5%
2017	33.7	24.8%
2018	41.3	22.6%
	10.37%	18.11%
CAGR RETURN	10.37%	
AVERAGE	18.11%	

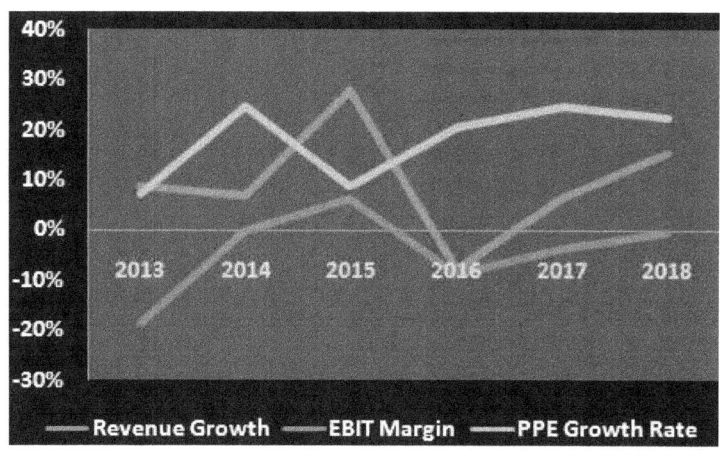

There is a strong relationship between three of them, in 2016 there is a degrowth in Revenue and EBIT around 8.9 % but then PPE has a growth of 20.5%

The Rate of Growth we can assume to be 8%

Expected Rate of Return for Apple Inc

```
Expected Rate of Return for Apple
  Distribution Yield = 9.13%
 +Rate of Growth    = 8%
                   = 17.13%
```

The expected return in investing in Apple Stock is 17.13%.

Organic Growth

The organic growth is due to the opening of stores, Apple has opened 506 retail stores across 24 countries, including 272 in the United States and 234 elsewhere, since May 2001,.Apple sale the product directly by their own store that include in revenue ,we can assure growth of 2 % from internal.

```
Expected Rate of Return for Apple
  Distribution Yield = 9.13%
 +Organic Growth    = 2%
                   = 11.13%
```

The expected return in investing in Apple Stock is 11.13%

Return on Leverage Ratio

Till now we have calculated the expected return from the investment in Apple stock, to know the exact return we can get from buying one stock of Apple, so we need to know the leverage ratio to get the number, by now we are calculating the expected rate of return buying the stock of Apple, and we are considering the debts potion of the balance sheet of Apple.

Now we will see what will be the return for investing in apple equity, in this case we need to know the leverage ratio then we need to get the interest cost, the cost of debts apple gets the fund.

The formula for Leverage Ratio:

Leverage = Debts / Equity

Interest cost = cost in percentage to get the debts funded.

Apple Leverage Ratio

Debts = $101 Billion
Market Cap = $1000
Leverage = $10.1%

Interest Cost = 4.5%

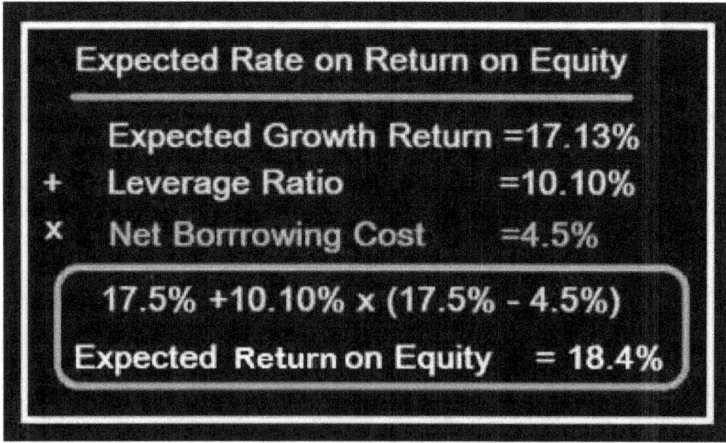

Expected Rate on Return on Equity

+ Expected Growth Return = 17.13%
× Leverage Ratio = 10.10%
  Net Borrrowing Cost = 4.5%

17.5% + 10.10% × (17.5% - 4.5%)
Expected Return on Equity = 18.4%

By investing 1$ in Apple Stock the expected return is 18.4%

After finding and understanding the company, we need to ask yourself, are we confident in our investment, this is what a value investor think.

The Value Chain

Value chain analysis typically includes two types of ventures:

- Firm value chain analysis (often referred to as Porter Value Chain Analysis) examines internal company practices and their optimization relative to creating value for customers.

- Industry value chain analysis involves examining the various stages of a product's production, from raw material procurement all the way through the final purchase by end-users.

A value chain includes profit and cost considerations for each step in a product's lifecycle, including raw material sourcing/production, manufacturing concerns and the characteristics of the final sale to end-users. During value chain analysis (VCA), each step (or "node") of a product's value creation is evaluated. These examined nodes include factors such as the sourcing of raw materials, costs associated with production and distribution, and the characteristics that drive customers' willingness to pay for the final product. Qualities of each node impact the total costs and expected margins of the final delivered product.
VCA is often used to identify opportunities for increased profit through the recognition of more

effective cost control, pricing, product positioning and/or distribution strategies.

At each node of the value chain, market participants are actively producing goods or offering services, while simultaneously making numerous choices that directly affect their profit margins.

In this case, the VCA details the profitability at several different nodes in the ice cream sales process, from raw material (dairy, sugar, flavorings) production, product manufacture, distribution and the final retail sale to the consumer. At each node, market participants experience unique cost and price considerations, and perform activities that add value above the material and labor inputs utilized, yielding varying gross profit margins.

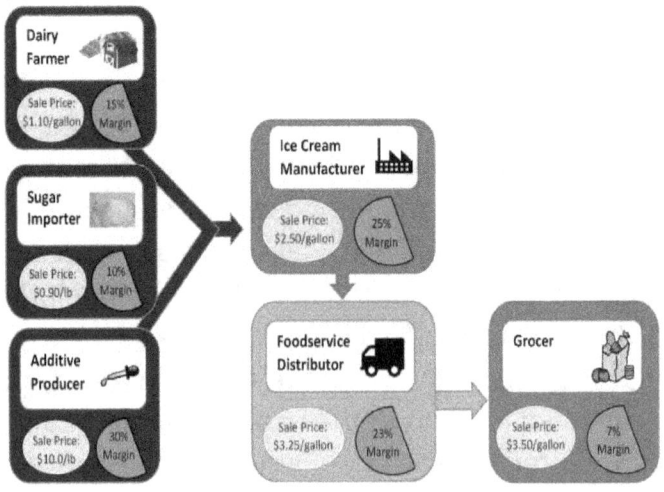

Value chain of Aviation Industry

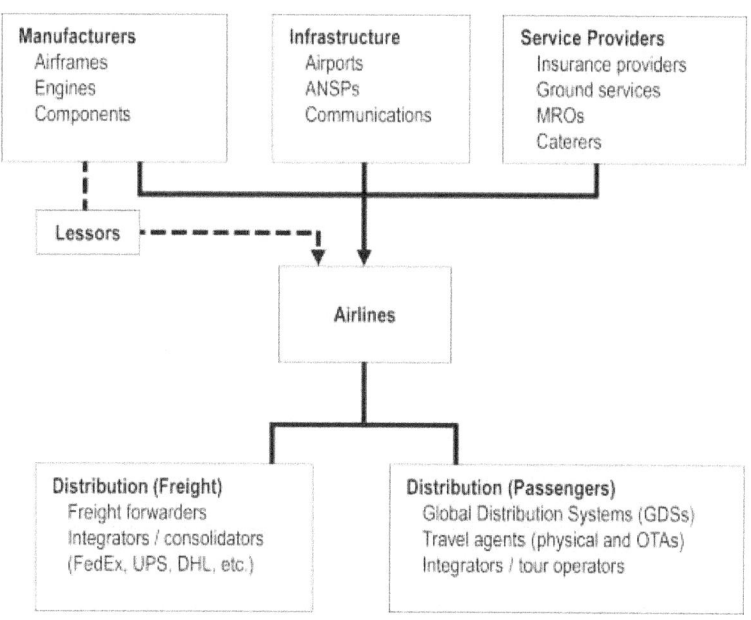

Value chain of Agricultural Industry

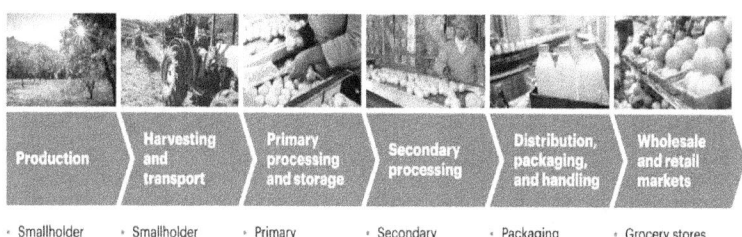

- The company is interconnected to with different company in a value chain.

- Like in aviation industry, if infrastructure cost increase, it will affect the margin of the airline industry.

- In a tractor company, if the farmer income decrease then, farmer will not able to buy the tractor, like if monsoon is not good then also that year tractor will sale will affect.

- Value chain applicable in all the company, suppose Apple sale there product to different country and of the import duty will increase in any country , the cost of the iPhone will increase , or else Apple have to absorbed the expenses and it will effect in operating margin

16

Debts & Cash

The Hidden Rule

Management with Debts and Cash

Issue Debts   Keep Cash

- Management issue corporate debts at very low interest rate, to fund the company.

- Management with good cash reserve do share repurchase, when they find the intrinsic value of the share is low, they restrict the liquidation of the shares floating with the market.

- Management with good cash, even issue the dividend to the shareholders, but some company don't issue any dividend as they have good opportunity available to invest and earn good return on the invested capital, such like Berkshire Hathaway never issue dividend as they invest to buy companies, whole company or potion of the company.

- Like apple issue corporate debts to buyback own shares and issue debts due to the cash fund is operating in the different part of the world, and they bring to united states, they need to pay taxes etc, so they issue low interest rate corporate debts.

- With good cash reserve, it might be little worried as, it's all depend on the management ability, they, might misuses it, with wrong investment like acquisition, we need to check what find of acquisition they did in the past and the corporate governess.

- Check the management stake in the company and not wasting cash in their leisure.

17
Risk Management

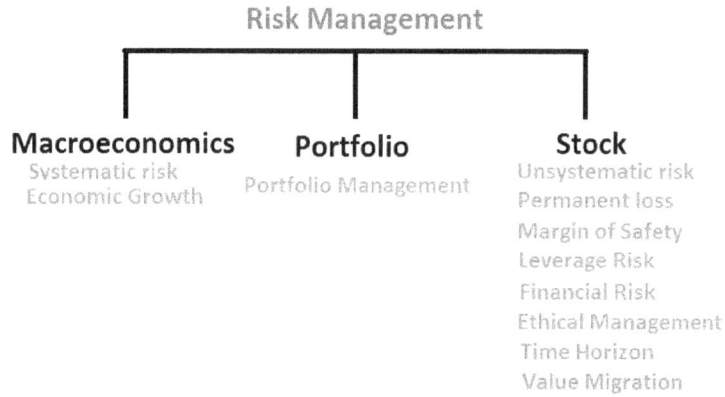

Risk is defined in financial terms as the chance that an outcome or investment's actual gains will differ from an expected outcome or return. Risk includes the possibility of losing some or all of an original investment.

Overall, it is possible and prudent to manage investing risks by understanding the basics of risk and how it is measured. Learning the risks that can apply to different scenarios and some of the ways to manage them holistically will help all types of investors and business managers to avoid unnecessary and costly losses.

Value investor don't use what MBA School teaches about risk and the calculation like" Quantifiably, risk is usually assessed by considering historical behaviors and outcomes. In finance, standard deviation is a common metric associated with risk. Standard deviation provides a measure of the volatility of asset prices in comparison to their historical averages in a given time frame".

Everyone is exposed to some type of risk every day – whether it's from driving, walking down the street, investing, capital planning, or something else. An investor's personality, lifestyle, and age are some of the top factors to consider for individual investment management and risk purposes. Each investor has a unique risk profile that determines their willingness and ability to withstand risk. In general, as investment risks rise, investors expect higher returns to compensate for taking those risks.

Beta is a measure used in fundamental analysis to determine the volatility of an asset or portfolio in relation to the overall market. The overall market has a beta of 1.0, and individual stocks are ranked according to how much they deviate from the market.

A stock that swings more than the market over time has a beta greater than 1.0. If a stock moves less than the market, the stock's beta is less than 1.0. High-beta stocks tend to be riskier but provide the potential for higher returns; low-beta stocks pose less risk but typically yield lower returns.

As a result, beta is often used as a risk-reward measure meaning it helps investors determine how much risk their willing to take to achieve the return for taking on that risk. A stock's price variability is important to consider when assessing risk. If you think of risk as the possibility of a stock losing its value, beta has appeal as a proxy for risk.

Value Investor doesn't use Beta and standard deviation to determine risk.

STOCK

Investing in the stock can be risky only when you have missed something to know about the company.

Margin of Safety

A principle of investing in which an investor only purchases securities when the market price is significantly below its intrinsic value. In other words, when market price is significantly below your estimation of the intrinsic value, the difference is the margin of safety. This difference allows an investment to be made with minimal downside risk. –*Investopedia*

A margin of safety is achieved when securities are purchased at prices sufficiently below underlying value to allow for human error, bad luck, or extreme volatility in a complex, unpredictable and rapidly changing world. – *Seth Klarman*

You have to have the knowledge to enable you to make a very general estimate about the value of the underlying business. But you do not cut it close. That is what Ben Graham meant by having a margin of safety. You don't try to buy businesses worth $83 million for $80 million. You leave yourself an enormous margin. When you build a bridge, you insist it can carry 30,000 pounds, but you only drive 10,000-pound trucks across it. And that same principle works in investing. – *Warren Buffett*

When you estimate the Earning Power Value to Market Value and when find there is a margin of safety then you buy the stock, margin of safety is determined towards your attitude of risk, but the number like 30 % is appropriate, your discipline is the most important towards the value investor, don't lower your standard, if you don't find the appreciate value, just do nothing.

When you do your search of finances value and you have calculated your expected return, don't invest in a company if you sure not sure what return it will deliver , in fact make sure what you have calculated expected return , the company must deliver that return .

Permanent Loss

- Loss comes when we don't know what is happening in the company, if you buy that kind of company where there is a corporate governance issue or there is a fraud happening in the company, after knowing this, if you still don't sell, the loses is compounding and you will lose all your capital invested in the company, that will be a permanent loss, don't love you stock that much , that you become bind to see something fraud is happening and you are not selling , where you suppose to sell, don't hold your stock too long to making money , late your loses move on , accept your mistake in investing .

- When operating margin is going down and inventory is increasing, then it indicates, something wrong happing in that industry or in company.

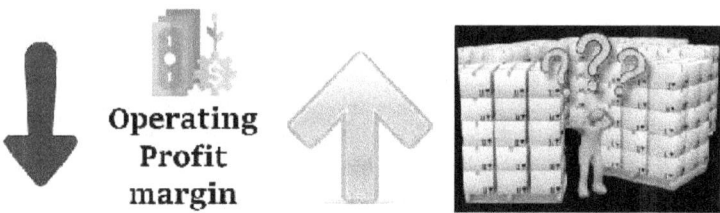

If this scenario company need more cash for the day today operating and might file for bankruptcy.

Value Migration

Value Migration is defined by Adrian Slywotzky, author of the book "Value Migration", as a flow of economic and shareholder value away from obsolete business models to new, more effective designs that are better able to satisfy customers' most important priorities. The framework tries to identify industries where Value Migration is underway and can help pick potential winners early in the cycle.

Typically, any business model exists in one of the three phases of Value Migration – Value Inflow, Stability or Value Outflow. Winning business models, as the name suggests, often find themselves in either inflow or stability phase. In the inflow phase, the industry or business captures value from other industries or businesses based on a superior consumer proposition. In the stability phase, the industry or business consolidates its position. In the value outflow stage, the incumbents witness share loss to businesses that are meeting customer needs more effectively. The report highlights case studies pertaining to all three phases of Value Migration.

Value Migration to some sector such as

- Automobiles - personal transportation shifted to service like Uber and Lyft.

- Bank - Payment banks shifted to PayPal and digital payment.

- Retail – Wal-Mart shifted to Amazon.

Ethical Management

- If the company operate in a very competitive industry and no barriers to entry then the management should take care of the operating profit and operating margin of the company, that will be the competence of the management to run a successful company in free industry, the cost structure to be low, else will be disappear.

- If the company enjoy barriers to entry and have a competitive advantage then, we want to see a management should be very focus on to protect the competitive advantage and barrier to entry.

Three kind of manager

- Efficient Manager
- Portfolio Manager
- Superior Manager

- *Efficient Manager*

    Efficient and Effectiveness as stated by Peter Drucker "Efficiency is doing things right; Effectiveness is doing the right thing." An organization survives based on the efficiency and effectiveness of a manager/management. Efficiency is the use of financial, human, physical and information resources such that output is maximised for any given set of resource inputs, or input is minimised for any given quantity and quality of output. An efficient manager might be doing the right job but not the job right. Doing the right job does not require much time or resource. A job can be done very quickly and efficiently within time. In this case, the manager's main aim is to get the job done within the allocated time using the given resources. But doing a job effectively involves time and planning the right strategy. In this case the manager concentrates more on the outcome rather than just the input. Both efficiency and effectiveness are an integral part of a successful management.

Management is almost entirely concerned with getting things done and determining how to get things accomplished. In each manager's mind there is a debate over whether more concern should go into low-cost production or to disregard production costs and go after complete satisfaction of goals and objectives. These two paths are known as the decisions which separate "Effectiveness" and "Efficiency." Effectiveness means that the job was done correctly and was accomplished but with no regard to whether the job was done inexpensively or on time. Whereas, efficiency means that the job was accomplished cheaply and on time yet may not be a very thorough and impressive accomplishment.

This manager is good for competitive industry.

- *Portfolio Manager*

    Conversely, a manager can take an active approach to investing; meaning that he attempts to consistently beat average market returns. In this scenario, the portfolio manager himself is extremely important, since his investment style directly results in the fund's returns. Potential investors should look at the active fund's marketing material for more information on the investment approach.

    They allocate capital such a way to generate the income above the cost of capital; they work like a portfolio manager such as Warren Edward Buffett is an American business magnate, investor, and philanthropist, who is the chairman and CEO of Berkshire Hathaway. He is considered one of the most successful investors in the world and has a net worth of US$88.9 billion as of December 2019, making him the fourth-wealthiest person in the world.

- *Superior Manager*

    A unique talent manager that can change the company into billions of dollar massive company such as Jeff Bezos CEO of Amazon, Tim Cook CEO of Apple and Elon Reeve Musk CEO of SpaceX and Tesla.

Leverage & Financial Risk

Leverage is often spoken of concerning the real estate market, but stock market leveraging is a practice often used by investors. The basic concept of leverage in the stock market, also called margin trading, involves borrowing capital to invest in more stock than what you can afford on your own. Stock market leverage can result in an increase in your return on investment, but you can lose more money than when buying stock using only your funds.

The primary risk associated with margin trading is the ability to lose a substantial amount of money in a short period of time. The fact that you borrowed money to invest in stock results in the possibility of losing more money than you personally put up to buy shares. The sale of assets in your account by the brokerage firm can result in additional losses. Understanding the margin agreement given to you by your broker and the rules of margin trading can help minimize risk.

To be a good value investor avoids Leverage.

Time Horizon

Benefits of Long-term Investment: One of the key factors that are associated with long term investment is lower volatility rate. Since, stocks are (highly) volatile, investing for longer period of time enables you to weather or sustain low market periods.

Putting your money in long-term rather than short-term investments also provide tax advantages on capital gains. Often long-term gains (those held over 12 months) are taxed at rates below your income tax bracket. Short-term gains, on the other hand, are taxed as regular income.

Portfolio

Portfolio Management

Is defined as the art and science of making decisions about the investment mix and policy, matching investments to objectives, asset allocation for individuals and institutions, and balancing risk against performance. Portfolio management is the art and science of selecting and overseeing a group of investments that meet the long-term financial objectives and risk tolerance of a client, a company, or an institution.

Portfolio management requires the ability to weigh strengths and weaknesses, opportunities and threats across the full spectrum of investments. When you buy a share, you are buying a portfolio of risk.

Type of risk in Managing a Portfolio

- Business Risk
- Customer Risk
- Supplier Risk
- Geographical Risk

- **Business Risk**

This kind of risk is the operation of business such as changes in the revenue, change in management, operating margin decline, fraud happen in company etc.

- **Customer Risk**

This risk comes from the customer side, like customer like and dislike, change in customer buying behaviour, change in customer income etc.

- **Supplier Risk**

Risk evolves in the price of raw material such as if the oil price increase that will affect in the changes in gas price and change in buying pattern of car, if interest rate change, if it goes high, might customer don't buy car.

- **Geographical Risk**

Company operate in different country as we have just seen in Apple, in that case there will be always a currency risk, if one country have any problem, then it will be effect the revenue of the company.

Portfolio Manager

There are some issues when your portfolio is managed by the portfolio manager, the risk as follows: -

- **Agency Issue** - The agency problem is a conflict of interest inherent in any relationship where one party is expected to act in another's best interests. In corporate finance, the agency problem usually refers to a conflict of interest between a company's management and the company's stockholders. The agency problem is a conflict of interest inherent in any relationship where one party is expected to act in another's best interests. In corporate finance, the agency problem usually refers to a conflict of interest between a company's management and the company's stockholders. The manager, acting as the agent for the shareholders, or principals, is supposed to make decisions that will maximize shareholder wealth even though it is in the manager's best interest to maximize his own wealth.

- The portfolio Manager should be specialised in the field of investing, the problem is that they are only specialised sector, might they be not able to look whole industry and pick great company.

- Diversification is important but be in limit, lots of diversification is a madness, issue is that portfolio manager can do the diversification for the sake of diversification, in which expend, mutual fund have diversification of around 100 stock and still they struggle for the returns, its madness.

Macroeconomics Risk

Macroeconomics is a branch of economics that studies how an overall economy—the market systems that operate on a large scale—behaves. Macroeconomics studies economy-wide phenomena such as inflation, price levels, rate of economic growth, national income, gross domestic product (GDP), and changes in unemployment.

Some of the key questions addressed by macroeconomics include: What causes unemployment? What causes inflation? What creates or stimulates economic growth? Macroeconomics attempts to measure how well an economy is performing, to understand what forces drive it, and to project how performance can improve.

There are two sides to the study of economics: macroeconomics and microeconomics. As the term implies, macroeconomics looks at the overall, big-picture scenario of the economy. Put simply, it focuses on the way the economy performs as a whole and then analyzes how different sectors of the economy relate to one another to understand how the aggregate functions. This includes looking at variables like unemployment, GDP, and inflation. Macroeconomists develop models explaining relationships between these factors. Such macroeconomic models, and the forecasts they produce, are used by government entities to aid in the construction and evaluation of economic, monetary and fiscal policy; by businesses to set strategy in domestic and global markets; and by investors to predict and plan for movements in various asset classes.

Assets Class Performance in Macroeconomics Risk

Low –   No Effect

Medium –   Equal to economic Effect

High -   Highly Effected

Risks	Real Estate	Stocks	Fixed Income	Franchises
Inflation	Low	Low	High	Low
Depression	Medium	High	High	Medium
Foreign exchange	High	High	High	Medium
Expropriation	High	High	Low	High
Recession	Low	Medium	Medium	Low
Deflation	Low	Low	Low	Low

Inflation - Inflation is a quantitative measure of the rate at which the average price level of a basket of selected goods and services in an economy increases over some period of time. It is the rise in the general level of prices where a unit of currency effectively buys less than it did in prior periods. Often expressed as a percentage, inflation thus indicates a decrease in the purchasing power of a nation's currency.

Economic Depression - In economics, a depression is a sustained, long-term downturn in economic activity in one or more economies. It is a more severe economic downturn than a recession, which is a slowdown in economic activity over the course of a normal business cycle.

Foreign Exchange - A firm has economic risk (also known as forecast risk) to the degree that its market value is influenced by unexpected exchange-rate fluctuations, which can severely affect the firm's market share with regard to its competitors, the firm's future cash flows, and ultimately the firm's value.

Expropriation is the act of a government claiming privately owned property against the wishes of the owners, ostensibly to be used for the benefit of the overall public. In the United States, properties are most often expropriated in order to build highways, railroads, airports, or other infrastructure projects.

A recession is a macroeconomic term that refers to a significant decline in general economic activity in a designated region. It had been typically recognized as two consecutive quarters of economic decline, as reflected by GDP in conjunction with monthly indicators such as a rise in unemployment. However, the National Bureau of Economic Research (NBER), which officially declares recessions, says the two consecutive quarters of decline in real GDP are not how it is defined anymore. The NBER defines a recession as a significant decline in economic activity spread across the economy, lasting more than a few months, normally visible in real GDP, real income, employment, industrial production, and wholesale-retail sales.

Deflation is a general decline in prices for goods and services, typically associated with a contraction in the supply of money and credit in the economy. During deflation, the purchasing power of currency rises over time.

Deflation causes the nominal costs of capital, labor, goods, and services to fall, though their relative prices may be unchanged. Deflation has been a popular concern among economists for decades. On its face, deflation benefits consumers because they can purchase more goods and services with the same nominal income over time.

However, not everyone wins from lower prices and economists are often concerned about the consequences of falling prices on various sectors of the economy, especially in financial matters. In particular, deflation can harm borrowers, who can be bound to pay their debts in money that is worth more than the money they borrowed, as well as any financial market participants who invest or speculate on the prospect of rising prices.

18

Important Note for Value Investor

- If you say that something is happening slowly but surely, you mean that it is happening gradually but it is definitely happening.

- As the saying goes, slow and steady wins the race, but where does this term come from? The origin is believed to be from one of Aesop's fables. Aesop was a Greek fabulist, and it's believed that he lived around the time of 620 to 560 B.C.E.

- "Success means being very patient, but aggressive when it's time."

- Being conservative, prudent, is a virtue not a defect.

- Look for a company which have moats, competitive advantages and barrier to entry.

- Look for a good company with good management to allocate capital.

- Don't buy in high multiple, but wait for the right time.

- Keep margin of safety always.

- A good value investor is willing to hold cash for an extended period of time because he finds nothing of value to invest in.

www.ingramcontent.com/pod-product-compliance
Lightning Source LLC
Chambersburg PA
CBHW071353210526
45465CB00001B/68